"I'm pleased to commend Mark Johnston's study of the Apostles' Creed. Written by a seasoned pastor as a guide for both individual and group study, it will prove especially useful at a time when an increase in doctrinal literacy within congregations is so much needed."

> —**Richard B. Gaffin Jr.**, Professor of Biblical and Systematic Theology, Emeritus, Westminster Theological Seminary, Philadelphia

"What do we believe? Our answer to that question will determine our eternity. The ancient creeds of the church are rooted in sacred Scripture, and they continue to provide the church in the twenty-first century with pertinent answers to our most significant spiritual questions. The Apostles' Creed is one of the church's earliest creeds, and while it continues to be recited in some congregations, it is neglected in most, if not altogether forgotten. With great pastoral care and scholarly insight, Mark Johnston calls our generation to return to the Apostles' Creed and to the historic confessional faith of our forefathers in order to preserve biblical fidelity and doctrinal orthodoxy for the next generation. This book will quickly prove to be an excellent tool for discipling Christians of all ages in the essential truths of the faith."

> —**Burk Parsons**, Associate Pastor of Saint Andrew's Chapel, Sanford, Florida, and Editor of *Tabletalk* magazine

"Wherever there is a dearth of historical knowledge or awareness, something old, such as the Apostles' Creed, is something new. This book is a welcome and much-needed encouragement for the church today. Because Mark Johnston brings years of pastoral experience and wisdom to an old creed, he resurrects timeless biblical truths that are foundational for a Christian or church to affirm. A careful study of these pages will instill confidence in any Christian who desires to knowledgeably answer that age-old question, 'What do you believe?'"

> —**K. Scott Oliphint**, Professor of Apologetics and Systematic Theology, Westminster Theological Seminary, Philadelphia

"The church would be hard-pressed to find a creed more important to her than the Apostles' Creed. She would also be hard-pressed to find a better, more practical exposition of it for her than *Our Creed*. In a length appropriate for a one-semester Sunday school class or Bible study, Mark Johnston has given the church a primer on essential theology loaded with probing, challenging study questions to drive that theology home. As I turned the last page, I found myself rejoicing again that my beliefs are neither provincial nor new. The Apostles' Creed reminds me that the truths I hold so dear are the same truths cherished by Christians around the world and throughout the centuries. I am grateful to God that I can join my voice with theirs in the words, 'I believe . . .'"

—**Mike Honeycutt**, Associate Professor of Historical and Practical Theology, Covenant Theological Seminary, St. Louis

"In this study of the Apostles' Creed, Mark Johnston reminds us both of the fundamental parameters and of the rich content of our evangelical faith. The good news of God's salvation is not about us, but about the glorious triune God who, through the death and resurrection of Jesus Christ, provided sinners with the way by which they can be reconciled to God and live in the hope of a future glory. That is the message of the Apostles' Creed, and I can think of no better guide to its content and grandeur than this book. I wish it a wide circulation."

—**Iain D Campbell**, Senior Minister, Point Free Church of Scotland, Isle of Lewis; Moderator of the General Assembly of the Free Church of Scotland, 2012

OUR
CREED

OUR
CREED

FOR EVERY CULTURE AND
FOR EVERY GENERATION

MARK G. JOHNSTON

P U B L I S H I N G
P.O. BOX 817 • PHILLIPSBURG • NEW JERSEY 08865-0817

ISBN: 978-1-59638-448-4 (pbk)
ISBN: 978-1-59638-589-4 (ePub)
ISBN: 978-1-59638-590-0 (Mobi)

Printed in the United States of America

Library of Congress Cataloging-in-Publication Data

Johnston, Mark G.
  Our creed : for every culture and for every generation / Mark G. Johnston.
      p. cm.
  Includes bibliographical references.
  ISBN 978-1-59638-448-4 (pbk.)
  1. Apostles' Creed. I. Title.
  BT993.3.J65 2013
  238'.11--dc23
                                    2012026855

for
Ian and Joan

Contents

Foreword

I don't usually look around our congregation during the worship services. But sometimes, especially at the beginning of a new academic year, I glance up early on in the service when one of my colleagues asks the congregation a question they hear every week: "Christians, what do you believe?"

That is the moment when I can tell who are new students, and whether or not they are used to our form of worship (for I know not every church sings the *Gloria Patri*, the Doxology, or even Psalms and hymns, or has a powerful organ accompanying the praise). And although we always mention that the response to the question "Christians what do you believe?" is printed in the worship bulletin, I still see expressions ranging from surprise to puzzlement.

Quietly I think to myself: "I know this is strange to you; someone has told you to come to our church because we are committed to the authority and exposition of God's Word. But there's more to worship than preaching. Stick with us, and in a few weeks or so you will be surprised that—perhaps for the first time in your life—you have learned by heart a summary of the Christian faith, almost without making the effort to memorize it."

The "answer" to the question "Christians, what do you believe?" is expressed (at our best, with energy, enthusiasm, and joy) in the words of the Apostles' Creed. We don't say it at every service (rarely, for example, at the evening service). We don't regard it as a matter of rote (any more than we regard singing "Great Is Thy faithfulness" or "In Christ alone" as

9

a matter of rote). Rather it is a constant reminder to us that there is substance to the Christian faith. The creed is a confession of what the Bible teaches us. It is a means of mutual encouragement. It is a confession of our faith in our great triune God, and the wonder of his work in creation, redemption, and consummation. We are reminded that the Christian life is not simply a matter of individual spiritual experience; it is anchored in truth. And every time we make this confession we remember that our church family is part of the immense world-wide and eternity-long family of pardoned sinners whom Christ has redeemed.

It is, as the subtitle of this little book suggests, a creed "for every generation."

So, even if the author, Mark Johnston, were not one of my longest-standing friends (he is—we have known each other for about thirty-five years!), I would be enthusiastic about *Our Creed: For Every Culture and for Every Generation*. The book is, after all, just the right length. It is written in an easy style. It shows us the relevance of an ancient confession for our contemporary lives. But I am all the more enthusiastic about it because it has been written by a man whose commitment to Christ, love for the church, enriching ministry of God's Word, and—not least—whose family life, have long been to me a blessing and an example to seek to follow.

Our Creed is a wonderful introduction to a creed used by Christians in all kinds of churches, whether its words are etched in marble in an ancient building where worship is formal and the music classical, or written on long colored banners hanging in functional buildings where hands rise in the air in response to new songs sung to the accompaniment of guitars and violins. I hope it will be widely read, and that those who read it will want to give copies to friends who are just beginning to find their way in the Christian life. But I also hope that some who have recited the words of the Apostles' Creed throughout their lives, but feel there is still something that eludes them, will, through these pages, find Christ in the creed.

For some readers, Mark Johnston is already an old friend. You have read some of his books, or perhaps had the pleasure of hearing him expound Scripture. For others, he will become a new friend through these pages. If you are in the latter category, I count it a special privilege to introduce him to you.

So now, read on!

Sinclair B. Ferguson
The First Presbyterian Church
Columbia, South Carolina

Preface

I t is almost automatically assumed that if we are looking for something fresh, then we need to look for the latest thing to appear on the shelf. That is true not just in the world of technology where the shelves are being restocked almost daily, but also in the realm of Christianity. Christians and churches are forever looking for the newest ideas and suggestions to revitalize their faith. The only problem with that approach to life—as our addiction to technology proves—is that the shelf life of what is new and fresh is getting shorter all the time. Life generally, and the Christian life in a more particular sense, needs resources that are richer and deeper and which have survived the test of time to sustain and guide us through the different circumstances we face. More often than not, it comes as a surprise to discover where those resources can be found. And that is where this little book comes in.

One resource that has been of the greatest help to Christian congregations for 1,500 years and more is the Apostles' Creed, but because it is so old (and so relatively brief) it has all too often been overlooked. So much so that almost every generation needs to discover it anew and realize—as so many others have before—that out of something so incredibly old, light that is remarkably fresh can brighten our understanding of the Bible and the way it applies to every age.

If you are already familiar with the creed, you might be forgiven for wondering how what I've just said could be true as you mentally scan the ancient wording once again. But it is not just that the details of its clauses have more to say than we often imagine; rather, the very shape and balance of the creed itself captures—in a way that has all too often been missed, especially by more recent generations of Christians—the shape and balance of the message of the Bible. And this structure is vital to grasping what the Bible's message is all about.

The instinct of many Christians today is to read the Bible as if it were "all about me." However, as the creed summarizes the biblical message, it makes clear that Scripture is actually "all about God." That doesn't mean that the Bible has nothing to say about us and our needs, but rather that we only truly begin to understand ourselves and our needs when we acknowledge God for who he is and how his purposes unfold. If we are Christians, simply recovering that balance in how we read and understand the Bible will in itself revitalize our faith, and that prospect is incentive enough to look more closely at the detail of this ancient summary of biblical teaching.

There is a very real sense in which the Apostles' Creed is, as my title suggests, "for every culture and for every generation" and really is "a creed for every generation." My prayer in writing this little commentary on the creed is that it will bring those who read it back to the deep roots of our faith and salvation in God himself. And, as it does so, that it will also provide that freshness that is so often missing from our lives—a freshness that is found not in some new idea, but in a rediscovery of those timeless truths that have been the heart of authentic Christianity down through the ages.

Mark G. Johnston
Proclamation Presbyterian Church
Bryn Mawr, Pennsylvania
April 2012

Acknowledgments

As is so often the case with books, the material in this volume went through a couple of different incarnations before it finally reached its present form. These pages began life as a series of sermons preached at the evening service in Grove Chapel, Camberwell, in London—the church I was privileged to pastor for some sixteen years. This material was intended to provide the congregation with a basic introduction to the major themes of the Bible's teaching. Shortly after the series began, I was asked to put it into written form for *Reformation 21*—the online magazine of the Alliance of Confessing Evangelicals (ACE). From there, with the kind permission and encouragement of those at ACE, it has now come into this more permanent form.

I will be forever grateful to the people of Grove Chapel for the opportunity to be their minister, not least because preaching to a congregation in one of the world's great melting pots of culture made me think afresh about the way the unchanging truths of Scripture relate to the ever-changing world in which we live. Sincere thanks are due as well to Derek Thomas and Gabriel Fluhrer of ACE for the opportunity, encouragement, and help they have given me in serving the wider cause of the gospel by having this book published. My appreciation also goes out to the Session and members of my present congregation in Bryn Mawr for their generous provision of study leave each year which allows me to serve the wider church in various ways, not least through writing.

In a very special way, however, these pages reflect the debt of gratitude I owe to Ian and Joan Hamilton and to a friendship that has been forged over many years through a number of unusual circumstances of life. Their wisdom, example, support, and prayers have been an enormous encouragement to me and to my family in the years that we have known them.

Study Guide

T he very nature of the Apostles' Creed as an ancient document that evolved and was refined over several hundred years of Christian thought means that its content deserves deeper and more extensive study than could be offered in a short commentary like this. Hence I have appended a set of study questions at the end of each chapter which are intended to encourage and facilitate further reflection on the creed and its teaching.

The study guide is designed either for individual use or as an aid for group study. Some questions in each section relate to what is covered in the appropriate chapter in the book. These intended to draw out a few of the key thoughts relating to the relevant statement from the creed. Other questions are intended to encourage wider (and hopefully, deeper) reflection and may involve some further reading. The list of additional material suggested for further reading (see page 123) ranges from small books right through to the very detailed two-volume commentary on the creed produced by Herman Witsius.

One vital point to bear in mind in going through these study questions is that they are meant to lead us back to Scripture to see where the teaching of the creed is rooted. For that reason, most of the questions are designed to explore specific verses or passages that underlie the particular teaching of the creed that is in view. All creeds, confessions, and catechisms are man-made summaries of the Bible's teaching; none of them can claim, as the Bible can, to be either inspired by God or free from error. Thus, they should be seen as tools to send us back to the Bible and help us study it more carefully.

Another thing to remember as we study the Bible and reflect on its teaching is that such study can never be an end in itself. An older generation of Christians used to say that "all truth is unto godliness" (picking up on Paul's comment about "truth" in the first verse of his letter to Titus). With that in mind, the questions in these studies will always include one or two that should encourage some thought and discussion about how these truths apply to our lives.

Finally—and most importantly—we need to keep in view that our exploration of the message of the Bible brings us face to face with God through Jesus Christ. This should lead us to worship and adore him. We often see this in the apostle Paul's writings where he has been explaining truths about God or salvation and he spontaneously bursts into praise. The more we see and learn of God, the more we should be thrilled by him and should respond to him—prayerfully, or in song—with praise and adoration.

If you intend to use this guide for group study, it will work most effectively if the group leader prepares the study in advance and comes with additional questions in mind that will help to stimulate discussion within the group. So too for group members: the more you are able to think about the questions in advance, the more you will be able to contribute to the discussion as well as benefit from the study.

The Apostles' Creed[1]

Although not written by the apostles, the Apostles' Creed is a concise summary of their teachings. It originated as a baptismal confession, probably in the second century, and developed into its present form by the sixth or seventh century.

I believe in God the Father Almighty,
    Maker of heaven and earth.

I believe in Jesus Christ, his only Son, our Lord,
    who was conceived by the Holy Spirit,
    and born of the virgin Mary.
    He suffered under Pontius Pilate,
    was crucified, died, and was buried;
    he descended into hell.
    The third day he rose again from the dead.
    He ascended into heaven
    and is seated at the right hand of God the Father Almighty.
    From there he will come to judge the living and the dead.

I believe in the Holy Spirit,
    the holy catholic church,
    the communion of saints,
    the forgiveness of sins,
    the resurrection of the body,
    and the life everlasting. Amen.

1. This version of the Apostles' Creed, with the accompanying introductory statement, is taken from *Trinity Hymnal*, rev. ed. (Suwanee, GA: Great Commission Publications, Inc., 1990), 845.

Who Needs a Creed?

W hen I was at primary school in the British state school system many years ago, it was still the norm not only to teach pupils the Apostles' Creed, but also to have them recite it in class. Looking back on that experience brings many thoughts to mind.

On the one hand, it is almost incredible to think that a state education system could require all pupils to learn such an overtly Christian statement of faith by heart. Such a thing would be inconceivable today—as much because it meant learning something by heart (or "by rote," as opponents of the practice like to say) as for the fact that it happened to be Christian. But on the other hand, the act of standing and reciting the creed had something of the feel that the daily act of pledging allegiance to the flag must have for many American school children. The words rolled off our tongues, but we had little or no understanding of their meaning or true appreciation of their significance. My guess is that the same is true for many churches where the practice of reciting the creed is still in vogue today. That raises the question, "Who needs a creed?"

The answer to that question from many in the broad sweep of Christendom would probably be, "Not us!" Such ancient documents are seen at best as outdated and at worst as irrelevant in an age that is more interested in the present than the past, and in which the very idea of beliefs that are fixed is tantamount to sacrilege. That may be the majority view—in a *de facto*, if not conscious sense—but that does not mean it is right. The church is always confessing its beliefs whether it realizes that to be the case or not; the issue is whether or not the beliefs we confess reflect those that are authentically Christian. There is a perennial need for such views to be challenged, ultimately for the sake of the gospel.

This point came home to me more than ever in the congregation and community I served on the edge of inner-city London. Within the church there was a wide cross section of people from all sorts of backgrounds. At one end of the spectrum were those who were well grounded in their faith after years of teaching and study. At the other end were those who came to Sunday services and mid-week groups but who had not the faintest clue of what Christianity is all about. And in between was everyone else! On top of that there was the local parish: a diverse community with all shades of religious belief, including no belief at all. People generally were suspicious about church—especially a church that had the word "evangelical" on its sign. So where were we to begin to address such an array of needs? It may come as more than a little surprise to learn that the Apostles' Creed provided a very useful tool—one that is able to help us understand and spread the gospel in all sorts of life circumstances. Let me suggest a number of ways in which that proves to be the case.

The Creed Helps Us Wrestle with the Challenge of Articulating the Faith

The very notion of "creed" immediately suggests the idea of expressing belief. In the barest sense it is an expression of truth in abstraction: "This is what Christians believe." But historically there was more to it than that. The Latin verb *credo*, from which "creed" is derived, carries a more personal and existential connotation. Hence, several major creeds begin with the words "I believe *in*"—in the sense of placing confidence in, or relying on, particular truths. The Apostles' Creed spells out the truths a person must believe in if he or she is to be a Christian.

The creed's history says a lot about its purpose. Even though legend had it that the original authors of this statement of faith were the twelve Apostles—each one contributing one of its twelve constituent parts—the reality is that it evolved from a number of earlier statements of faith. The main antecedent was the so-called Old Roman Creed; but that in turn seems to have been an evolution of two other documents: the *Epistula Apostolorum* and what has come to be known as *Der Bazileh* papyrus—probably part of an Egyptian communion liturgy. Each of these in their own historical settings was an attempt to articulate the faith crisply and clearly for seekers and catechumens.

Those who framed these various statements of faith were simply following the pattern found in Scripture itself. From the simplest article of faith found in the Great *Shema*—"Hear, O Israel, the LORD our God, the LORD is one" (Deut. 6:4)—right through to the *Carmen Christi* of Philippians 2, the Bible offers multiple examples of summaries and confessions of its own teachings. In this the Bible shows us that its teaching has to be systemized if it is to make sense to us.

Church historian Philip Schaff, in his magisterial *The Creeds of Christendom*, quotes Martin Luther commending the Apostles' Creed by saying, "Christian truth could not possibly be put into a shorter and clearer statement." Schaff himself comments, "As the Lord's Prayer is the Prayer of prayers, the Decalogue the Law of laws, so the Apostles' Creed is the Creed of creeds."[1] The challenge the creed presents to the church in the twenty-first century is to use it as a framework for expressing these time-honored truths that are essential to Christian faith for the world of our day.

The Creed Provides a Tool for Teaching the Faith

It has been said that the Apostles' Creed was the Alpha course, or Christianity Explored course of its day. That isn't far from the truth. Successive generations have come up with their own tools for presenting the main teachings of the Bible, but the Apostles' Creed is the mother of them all. It sets the principle and provides a paradigm for what needs to be taught.

J. I. Packer's book *I Want to Be a Christian*[2] is a fairly recent example of how the creed can continue to function as an effective teaching tool in a contemporary church setting. Packer uses the creed as a framework for exploring each tenet of the faith in such a way as to lead young Christians to see the essence of what is meant, while at the same time providing pointers for those who want to dig deeper.

At an even more basic level, the simple practice of memorizing the creed and reciting it publicly still has enormous merit—especially in an age when memorizing anything is deemed passé. In the syllabus of what every child ought to learn by heart, the Apostles' Creed must take its place as a core component alongside the list of books of the Bible, Ten Commandments, and the Lord's Prayer. And if adults haven't got there yet, it's never too late to start.

The creed is a wonderfully versatile tool for instruction. It has a use with children, seekers, new converts, and those who realize that no matter how long we may have been in the

---

1. Philip Schaff, *The Creeds of Christendom, with a History and Critical Notes*, 3 vols. (1877; repr., Grand Rapids: Baker, 1993). Schaff's comment can be found at 1:14. Luther's quote appears at 1:15n2.

2. J. I. Packer, *I Want to Be a Christian* (Eastbourne, UK: Kingsway Publications, 1977).

faith, we can always discover new depths even in the most familiar truths.

The Creed Makes Us Focus on the Heart of the Faith

There is always a temptation to get lost in the minutiae of what the Bible teaches—as is seen in all too many of the distractions and controversies of the New Testament church and the church generally throughout its history. Nowhere was this tendency more damaging than in the church at Corinth, and the apostle Paul's response to such distractedness is timeless. He reminds Corinthians of what he had taught them in the first place: "What I received I passed on to you as of first importance" (1 Cor. 15:3)—here are the core teachings that form the bedrock of the Christian Faith.

So as the creed spells out the sum of saving knowledge for the early church, it takes us first and foremost to the God of the Bible in all his uniqueness and glory. His uniqueness lies in the fact that he is Trinity and his greatest glory is seen in the salvation he provides at such extraordinary cost through his own Son. Grasping this is the theological equivalent of finding the "holy grail" of science: the theory of everything (except that theology seeks to express not a theory, but the God-given truth that is the key to everything).

In an age when evangelical Christianity is rapidly losing its way in a maze of "steps to salvation" and myriad books and sermons on the "how to" of the Christian life, the creed brings us back to the heart of both the gospel and the faith: God himself.

The Creed Guards the Gospel against Distortions of the Faith

Historically, creeds have had a double function: to serve as both a fence and a foundation. They serve as the latter in that they crystallize the essence of all a person needs to know for life and salvation—that inevitably is more than just a "simple gospel." In that sense creeds provide a foundation for the church, since the church is the community of the redeemed and is built on the teaching "of the apostles and prophets with Christ Jesus himself as the chief cornerstone" (Eph. 2:20). The Apostles' Creed encapsulates positively what the essence of that teaching is.

The sad reality of course is that the community of the redeemed has been plagued not merely from without, but more often from within by distortions of that teaching. So creeds have been formulated to provide a fence to guard the church against such aberrations. It is noteworthy that the most insidious distortions of the faith that threatened the church in the early centuries of its existence concerned the doctrine of God himself—whether as Trinity, or in the mystery of the incarnation. It is understandable, therefore, that the Apostles' Creed is particularly concerned to secure that fence, given the era in which it was framed.

It would be nice to think that almost twenty centuries later, the church no longer needs to go over these elementary teachings of the faith again; but it does. Whether through the assault of open theism or well-meaning ignorance, the truths enshrined in the creed still need to be guarded, and the creed itself continues to be a most effective way to do so.

The Creed Shows the Need for Personal Faith

In every generation, perhaps the greatest threat to the church and the teachings on which she stands is that of the slide into nominalism. Paul warns Timothy that the Last Days will be characterized by those (in the church) who have a "form of godliness" but who deny its power (2 Tim. 3:5). He warns against these people in the strongest possible terms.

26

This is a danger that lurks most subtly in the Reformed community, where we are inclined to lay great store on scholarship and precision. Such an environment can be paradise for the kind of people Paul is warning us about—especially those who delight in controversy. The essence of Christianity that is authentically Reformed is its concern for authentic experience. The experiential Calvinism of the Reformation and Puritan eras was driven by the conviction that all truth leads to godliness. The study of theology can never be merely academic.

The first three words of the Apostles' Creed embed that conviction at the very centre of the truths it goes on to confess. It is only as we declare our belief *in* this God and all that he has done that we can actually know him along with all the benefits he promises in the gospel. There is a piety reflected in the creed that is key to understanding its truths and making them live for the church and all its members: the piety of genuine personal faith.

STUDY QUESTIONS

Many times in Christian history people have used the slogan, "No Creed but the Bible!" At face value this sounds very commendable—not least because all too often the statements of faith produced by churches have either been born out of disagreements, or have caused them. How, then, can we justify documents like the Apostles' Creed?

This opening study will not only provide the opportunity to think about and discuss that question, but will also point to some key passages in the Bible that help to answer the question more directly.

1. How would you respond to someone who used the slogan, "No Creed but the Bible"?

2. Look up 2 Timothy 1:13–14. Paul has just spoken of his role as a "herald, apostle and teacher" of the gospel (v. 11) and he now describes the essence of what he has taught Timothy as "the pattern of sound teaching."

   a. Why does Paul say that his teaching is "sound"? (The word he uses also means "healthy.")
   b. Why does he describe it as the "*pattern* of sound teaching"?
   c. How should this help Christians to be alert to interpretations of the Bible that are unsound?
   d. Why does this pattern of teaching need to be kept "with faith and love in Christ Jesus"?
   e. Paul also calls this pattern of teaching "the good deposit": why does Timothy (and why do Christians through the ages) need the Holy Spirit's help to guard this deposit?
   f. In what sense is the Apostles' Creed a "pattern of sound teaching"?

3. Look up 2 Timothy 2:2. Paul is still talking about the essence of the teaching he has passed on to Timothy but now speaks of how that same teaching is to be passed on through the generations that follow.

   a. What did it mean for Timothy to "entrust to reliable men" what he had heard Paul teach publicly?
   b. Why was it important for these men not only to be "reliable" but "qualified to teach others" as well?
   c. How do summaries of the main elements in the Bible's teaching like the Apostles' Creed help us to pass on the heart of the Christian message from generation to generation?

4. In what ways does the creed function as a "fence and a foundation" for the core teachings of the Bible?

5. Given that the Bible ranges far and wide in what it says, how does the creed help us to identify and articulate the main components of its message?

6. Why is it important to notice that the creed begins with the words "I believe *in* . . ."?

The God of the Creed

"I believe in God!" So what? Don't most people? The number of real atheists in the world and throughout history is pretty small. So what's so special about these opening four words of the Apostles' Creed? The answer, of course, is what lies behind them.

If you met a woman in the street who was dressed in black from head to toe, with only a slit in a veil for her eyes to look out, and heard her say, "I believe in God," you would know exactly which god she had in mind. The same would be true for a troupe of saffron-robed, drum-beating Krishna-chanters. The context controls the meaning of the words we use.

The Christian context in which the wording of this creed evolved immediately colors the way in which we understand what it says. The God of the creed is the God of the Bible. So, as we skim through the way the creed goes on to articulate who God is and what he is like, it becomes immediately apparent that he is the God who is Trinity. The comma after "God" in the first line paves the way for the unfolding of the precise nature of God in what follows: namely, that he is Father, Son, and Holy Spirit.

The Starting Point

All this raises the question of where we start as we try to articulate the Christian Faith. Many great statements of faith—the Westminster Confession of Faith being the greatest of them all—begin with a statement about the Bible; but others begin with a statement about God. Is one to be preferred above the other?

Those that begin with a statement about the Bible do so in the conviction that God cannot be known apart from the Bible. So, before we can have a meaningful doctrine of God, we need a meaningful doctrine of Scripture. Theology is not a construct of man's ideas about God, but rather an expression on what God has made known about himself. To try to piece together an understanding of God in the abstract as a mere philosophical exercise is a mission doomed to failure. As Zophar says to Job, who can "by searching find out God?" (Job 11:7 KJV). Christianity is at its very core a religion of revelation.

Of course, those who framed the other classic statements of faith that begin with God and not Scripture would not for a moment disagree. The reasoning behind their order is equally valid and compelling: namely, that you cannot have a Bible without the God who gave it. But what is clear is that the God they confess is the God who has made himself known in the Bible and who can neither be defined nor understood apart from it.

In that sense the issue of where to start in our formulation of what we believe as Christians is something of a moot point between friends! The framers of the Apostles' Creed opted for the latter starting point in the knowledge that their source is not human reason, but the divine self-revelation in Scripture.

Beyond All Comprehension

Whichever starting point we choose, it is clear, as we have said, that the God who is there and the God who has made himself known in the Bible is the God who is Trinity. He is one God in three Persons. This is the quintessential distinguishing mark of the Christian religion, and what is so striking about it is the fact that it is beyond all human comprehension.

That in itself is telling. If the Bible was of merely human origin and the God of the Bible an elaborate invention of religious minds, then why come up with such a view of God? The very notion of a God who is simultaneously one in three and three in one borders on the absurd and takes us beyond the realm of what is naturally believable. The only explanation for such a view of God being at the very heart of Christian theism is that it reflects what he reveals about himself in his Word.

The sheer difficulty of formulating the doctrine of God as he is revealed in the Bible is seen in the fact it took almost four centuries of debate within the church for a consensus to crystallize. But what was clear as that debate unfolded and in the subsequent challenges its conclusion has faced is that it isn't merely the Bible's *view* of God that is inescapably Trinitarian, but rather its *entire message*.

Given the weight of importance attached to this doctrine by the early church and even more so its pervasiveness throughout the message of the Bible, it seems strange that the doctrine of the Trinity has such a low profile in Christian understanding and in so much of today's preaching. But then again, perhaps that explains something of the "weightlessness of God" bemoaned by David Wells in so much contemporary evangelicalism.[1]

God's Fingerprints

Having said that the Bible is the source of Trinitarian theology, when we begin to understand what that means, we realize that this Trinitarian God has left his fingerprints all

1. See Wells's *God in the Wasteland* (Eerdmans, 1994) for more on this concept.

over his creation. Rather like the way in which someone who has just been inducted to the nuances and subtleties of the world of fine art is suddenly able to recognize a Matisse or a Renoir from the artist's brush strokes, the person whose eyes have been opened to see God as he is made known in his Word begins to see the world in different light.

David captures this eloquently in Psalm 19 when he says, "The heavens declare the glory of God; the skies proclaim the work of his hands" (Ps. 19:1). Or again in Psalm 29—reworked, apparently, from an ode to Baal—"The voice of the LORD is over the waters; the God of glory thunders" (Ps. 29:3). Even pagans perusing the world and universe in which they live are confronted with hints and glimpses of the God who is their maker. David goes further again in Psalm 139 to speak of the mystery of his own humanity: "I praise you because I am fearfully and wonderfully made" (Ps. 139:14). There is no true self-understanding that can be separate from an understanding of God. Shakespeare picks up this thought in the words that he places on Hamlet's lips:

> What a piece of work is a man, how noble in reason, how infinite in faculties, in form and moving how express and admirable, in action how like an angel, in apprehension how like a god!
>
> — *Hamlet*, Act 2, Scene 2

Or, to use John Frame's expression, "We live in a sacramental universe."[2] Creation itself points us to God; but does it lead us to anything more than mere theism?

Paul says that it does. In his exposition of general revelation, from which he goes on to expound the gospel in its fullness, he speaks of God's making himself known in the

---

2. This idea is explored more fully in Frame's *Worship in Spirit and Truth* (Phillipsburg, NJ: P&R Publishing, 1996).

created order to such an extent that his "invisible qualities—his eternal power and divine nature—have been clearly seen, being understood from what has been made . . . so that they are without excuse" (Rom. 1:20). It's hard not to infer from that final caveat that Paul has more than bare theism in mind in terms of where general revelation leads. Sufficient knowledge of God can be gleaned from the book of creation that sets him apart from the multitude of pagan deities that have come and gone through history.

That means that there is more than a hint of God's Trinitarian character in the world and universe he has made. As suggested in the previous chapter, the scientific quest for a "theory of everything"—something that explains the unity within diversity that surrounds us in the cosmos—resonates with what the Bible says about the God who created all things and the inevitable stamp of his character impressed on all he has made.

This facet of the doctrine of the Trinity has massive relevance not only for how theology interacts with science, but, more significantly, for how the gospel engages with the world. The Trinity is a vital key to mission in terms of how it challenges false views of God that abound and also provides a credible answer to the unity-diversity conundrum that so vexes the postmodern mind.

The Unfolding Mystery

Robert Letham, in his *magnum opus* on the Trinity,[3] compares the unfolding mystery of God's nature and character in the Bible to a detective novel. Only after having progressed some way through the book does the reader find him or herself drawn back to details that were both striking and baffling at earlier stages; now one can actually understand what these

3. See Robert Letham, *The Holy Trinity: In Scripture, History, Theology, and Worship* (Phillipsburg, NJ: P&R Publishing, 2004).

details mean. So it is with what we see and learn of God in the progress of revelation in Scripture.

The oddities of the language used in relation to God in the opening chapters of Genesis—plural nouns used with singular verbs, a singular God saying, "Let us make"—leave any student of the Bible wondering what kind of God this is. These bizarre ascriptions continue throughout the Old Testament in ways that unsettled even Jewish rabbis; but it is only when we enter the realm of New Testament revelation that the lights begin to come on.

As Jesus steps into our world in human flesh—the One in whom the "fullness of the godhead dwells in bodily form," who could say, "Whoever has seen me has seen the Father," and who could speak of sending the Holy Spirit—the revelation of God reaches its zenith as far as this present world is concerned. So when Jesus sends his disciples into the world to do his work, he tells them to baptize the nations "in the name" that is simultaneously one yet three. And when his apostles bless his people they do so with that same formula.

It has been rightly said that there is no fully developed theology of the Trinity in the New Testament; but there are enough clues not only there, but throughout the whole Bible, to compel the church to this doctrine as being the only way to express what God is like as we meet him in his Word. The Apostles' Creed is a judicious expression of that truth that has served the church well for most of its history.

The God of Our Salvation

Two big questions hang over any doctrine that we glean from Scripture: "Why is it important?" and "What difference does it make?" There is probably no doctrine to which these questions are more pertinent than that of the Trinity.

At one level the answer to the first of these questions is simply, "Because it's there and because it's true!" Just as we must accept our fellow men as they are and not as some projection of what we would like them to be, so too we can do no other than accept God as he has made himself known in the Bible. Even though we often hear people say, "Well, this is how I like to think of God," their wistful imaginings are a total irrelevance alongside the realities God has revealed.

When it comes to the second question, its relevance is most pertinent with relation to understanding salvation. In a broad sense there is a Trinitarian flavor to all that is said about salvation throughout the New Testament. The great confession of Jonah—"Salvation is of the LORD" (Jonah 2:9 KJV)—opens up into its full splendor when we see that salvation is intricately bound up with the planning, accomplishment, and application of the triune Father, Son, and Spirit. That's what puts the "great" into the "great salvation" found in Hebrews!

The God in whose image we are made is the same God by whom we are remade so that his image will be perfectly restored in our collective as well as individual identities.

So when the architects of the creed chose to begin with the words, "I believe in God"—with all that this implies with regard to the God of the Bible—they were simply pointing to the God who is most worthy of our trust and confidence as we look to him for salvation. More than that, he is the God who is uniquely able to help us make sense of ourselves and of the world and universe in which he has placed us. The more we know him, the more we are liberated to not only honor him, but also to enjoy him forever!

STUDY QUESTIONS

It would be easy to think that it is only in our world that the statement "I believe in God . . ." needs to be punctuated by the question, "Which God?" The world in which the Apostles'

Creed was born was just as much a world of many gods and many faiths as our own. In light of that, it is not merely astonishing, but significant that the creed sees no need to qualify or justify its opening declaration about God. The Christian context in which it was written shapes and molds the understanding of the Bible truths it conveys.

This study will focus on the uniqueness of the God of the Bible and especially the ways in which he has made himself known.

1. In what ways might the statement "I believe in God" become a useful starting point for discussion, either with someone who is not yet a Christian or a group of people from different backgrounds?

2. Look up Psalm 19:1–6. In this psalm, David praises God for the ways he makes himself known, beginning with the way he has revealed himself in the world and universe he has created.

   a. David uses a number of words to show how God communicates through the things he has made. In what sense does God "speak" through the created order?
   b. How far does this self-revelation of God reach, and what does that mean for people who have never had the opportunity to read the Bible?
   c. Why is it significant that the "glory" of God is displayed in what he has made (v. 1)?

3. Look up Romans 1:18–23. In this opening chapter of Romans, Paul picks up on the theme of how God reveals himself in what he has made, only now he teases out the moral and spiritual implications this has for everyone.

   a. What does Paul mean when he speaks of men "who suppress the truth by their wickedness" (v. 18)?

b. Why does God have every right to reveal his wrath against such people (vv. 19–21)?
c. What is the particular sin for which God holds them accountable (vv. 22–24)?
d. Why is this "general revelation" God has given of himself enough to leave people "without excuse" before him, but not enough to save them?

4. Look up Psalm 19:7–14. David completes his song of praise for the way God has made himself known by speaking of his written Word, the Bible.

   a. How do these verses help us to understand how God makes himself known in his written Word?
   b. How do these verses help us to understand how God makes the way of salvation known in his written Word?

5. Look up Matthew 28:19–20 and 2 Corinthians 13:14. How do these verses help us to realize that the God of the Bible is one God in three Persons and so is different from the gods of other religions?

That God Should Come as One of Us!

I t is one of best-known facts of the Bible; yet it is shrouded in mystery. Its details are rehearsed every year in preaching, reading, and song; yet they defy our comprehension. The virgin birth—or, more accurately, the virginal conception—of the Lord Jesus Christ is the point at which the transcendence and immanence of God converge, and they do so in a way that defines the destiny of the universe. The sheer wonder of it all is well captured in the words of a Graham Kendrick hymn:

> O what a mystery I see, what marvelous design,
> That God should come as one of us, a Son in David's line.
> Flesh of our flesh, of woman born, our humanness he owns;
> And for a world of wickedness, his guiltless blood atones.[1]

In a stroke Kendrick captures the marvel of the incarnation and at the same time signals why it matters and where it

---

1. Graham Kendrick, "O What A Mystery I See," © 1988 Make Way Music (admin. by Music Services in the Western Hemisphere). All Rights Reserved. ASCAP. Used by permission.

ultimately leads. And that's where the Apostles' Creed takes us in its next major clause. Having confessed our belief in the God of the Bible, the creed goes on to say, "I believe in Jesus Christ his only Son, our Lord; who was conceived by the Holy Spirit, born of the Virgin Mary." It is, as Karl Barth has said, the great miracle that stands guard at the beginning of Christ's earthly life and ministry and the salvation it would accomplish, counterbalanced at the other end of his life and work by the miracle of the resurrection.

Seen in those terms, Tolkien fans cannot help but be reminded of the scene at Moria Gate in *The Fellowship of the Ring*. Frodo and his little band are hopelessly hemmed in on every side: the mountains are in front of them, too high and wide to traverse or circumvent; their enemies are behind them; and a sinister creature is lurking in the lake beneath them. But before them stands Moria Gate, the supernatural portal that guards the path through the mines to safety on the other side. It is their only hope of escape.[2] But in the real world it is the supernatural conception of Jesus that is the true gate that guards the path to human salvation and glory beyond!

The language employed by the creed is carefully chosen, giving on the one hand the Lord's earthly name, "Jesus"—which designates him as God's promised Savior—while at the same time including what J. I. Packer calls his "official name"—the title "Christ." This highlights the threefold office of Prophet, Priest, and King through which we discover what salvation entails: knowing God, being reconciled to him, and submitting to his saving, sovereign rule. Given that these offices had been in existence for millennia among God's people, but could do no more than give a preview of God's plan of redemption, we begin to appreciate why they take on a whole new significance when all three are occupied by the One who is not only "Jesus

2. In case anyone needs a reminder, this exciting adventure occurs in book 2, chapter 4, of Tolkien's classic work, which is easily available in many fine editions.

Christ" but also God's "only Son, our Lord." God's Savior, the Jesus of history, is none other than his Son from eternity! He is the Son who not only entered our world in a unique way, but did so by becoming the unique Person who is uniquely qualified to bring the salvation God had promised and which our race so desperately needs.

God had already dropped astonishing hints which flagged in advance the uniqueness of both this Person and his coming. Isaiah has many references to the promised Messiah which leave little doubt as to the divine dimension to his being and the manner of his coming into the world. The "sign of Immanuel" (Isa. 7:14), speaking of a virgin who "will be with child," is one, and the extraordinary child with the names of God (Isa. 9:6) is another. But all these previews seemed too amazing to be true—as Peter said after the event: "Even angels long to look into these things" (1 Peter 1:12). It is only when we reach the Gospels that we discover the denouement that these earlier hints had promised. First, with the eyewitness accounts of Matthew and Luke—which included testimony from Mary herself—we get the bare miraculous facts (Matt. 1:18–21; Luke 1:26–38; 2:1–7). Then in John we get the breath-taking explanation: "The Word became flesh and made his dwelling among us" (John 1:14). The eternal Logos introduced in the opening words of John's prologue is the Jesus expounded in the Gospel that follows—the Son of God in human flesh!

From the perspective of the twenty-first century "Christian" West, people might be forgiven for thinking, "Why does all this stuff really matter?" It makes for a cute story that is retold and re-enacted Christmas after Christmas. It also makes for great music, as box-office takings of Handel's *Messiah* bear testimony year after year. But is there more to it than that?

The angels of heaven must tear their hair out (metaphorically) as the great truths of Handel's oratorio sit like feathers on the minds and hearts of its hearers. So too as countless parents look on with glowing admiration for their child's performance of the Nativity, but with little or no appreciation of the events it represents. But then must they not be even more exasperated by preachers who do so little to open the eyes of their congregations to the awesome wonder of what took place when Jesus came?

The sad corollary of all this is a view of "Christian" salvation evacuated of all credible substance—a view that becomes but a variation on the theme of "salvation from below" that is shared by every other world religion. The uniqueness of the Christian gospel hinges on the uniqueness of Christ the Savior it proclaims—a uniqueness captured majestically by John at the beginning of his Gospel as "salvation from above" through a Savior who has come literally from another world to bring deliverance. There are at least three things in John's summary of the incarnation that not only spell out its glory (which John saw), but also hold the key to its gospel hope in the One of whom he speaks.

A Savior Who Has the Capacity to Save

When we hear John say, "the Word became flesh," it is of course the Word to whom we have been introduced in the opening lines of the Gospel. The same Word who "was God and who was with God," who in the beginning simply "was" (John 1:1). The limitations of language struggle to express the depth and wonder of the eternal realities John has in mind, the mystery of God himself.

John uses the language of deity in relation to the Word/Logos: most obviously that he "was God." But more than that, John says quite simply that when time began, the Word already "was"—he already had existence, he was the being One. Or, to put it another way, the underived existence that is God's by nature also belongs to the Logos. The Word is God.

John also uses the language of relationship: "the Word was with God." In the Greek John uses the expression *pros ton theon*, which might be translated more literally, the Word was "toward" God in eternal relationship—turned out from himself toward another in perfect loving devotion. Although of necessity equal with God [the Father], because he shares the same essential deity, he nevertheless devotes himself to God.

This is the "Word" who "became flesh." He is none other than the eternal Son of God—spoken of again by John three chapters later when he says, "For God so loved the world that he gave his one and only Son" (John 3:16). It was the second Person of the godhead who, in the womb of the Virgin Mary, was joined mysteriously to her "flesh," sharing her DNA, and bringing into being the God-man. As Donald MacLeod has put it, Jesus' human nature was "created, not *ex nihilo*, but *ex Maria*."[3]

In that extraordinary nanosecond in history, the infinity and eternity of God was joined to all the limitations of space and time in our humanity. He was made like us in everything apart from our sin. But in that instant as well, there came into existence the only Person with the capacity to do what God required to usher in salvation.

That incredible capacity began to shine through as Jesus embarked upon his earthly ministry. The man from Nazareth had the ability to heal the sick, feed the hungry, control the elements, walk on water, and even raise the dead. So astonishing was he that not only was he mobbed by curious crowds, but also the more discerning among them asked the question, "Who is this? Even the wind and waves obey him!" (Mark 4:41). It is the question which is finally answered at Caesarea Philippi when Peter makes the astounding confession, "You are the Christ, the Son of the living God" (Matt. 16:16). Behind the veil of a finite humanity lies the infinite capacity of God himself.

The full weight of significance bound up with that fact only becomes apparent on the cross. When Jesus goes to his

3. Donald McLeod, *The Person of Christ* (Downers Grove, IL: IVP Academic, 1998), 42.

death as the "Lamb of God who takes away the sins of the world" (John 1:29), the only way his sacrifice can provide an atonement of global and pan-historical dimensions is if he is more than just a man. In terms of equivalence, the death of a single human being who was perfect in every way would secure the salvation of another single human being; but no more. It is only because Jesus is not merely man, but God-man that he has the capacity to redeem the great multitude who will be with him in glory. To borrow from Barth, we can say that he came as God for man.

A Savior Who Has the Authority to Save

We are entitled to ask, "What gives Jesus the authority to promise salvation to those who trust him?" After all, the world throughout its history has been full of self-appointed "saviors" who are just that: "self-appointed'—they have no authority to actually provide what they claim to offer.

In one sense the question has been answered already in what we have said about Jesus' being "*God* in human flesh," but there is more to it. His authority to act as Savior also resides in the fact that he is "God *in human flesh*"—he had to become one of us. And that's exactly what John tells us: "The Word became flesh"—he took *human* flesh, not that of some other life-form. He might have come as an angel—which to our minds might have seemed more dignified and appropriate—but if that had been so he could not have saved us.

The writer of Hebrews puts his finger on it when he says in relation to a salvation that is genuine and will deliver what we need:

> Since the children have flesh and blood, he too shared their humanity so that by his death he might destroy him who holds the power of death—that is, the devil—and free those who all their lives were held in slavery by their fear of death. For

46

surely it is not angels he helps, but Abraham's descendants. For this reason he had to be made like his brothers in every way, in order that he might become a merciful and faithful high priest in service to God, and that he might make atonement for the sins of the people (Heb. 2:14–17)

Jesus' authority to save resides in the fact that he is not merely God sent from God, but that he is sent as man who corresponds perfectly to those he came to save and to their need. All that we are not, he is, and everything we are incapable of doing, he does. The good news of the gospel is not merely that Jesus came as God for man, but that he also came as perfect man for God!

A Savior Who Can Be Trusted to Save

The great unspoken implication of what the creed goes to such pains to express is that only such a Savior can truly save! But what the creed does not articulate, John does in the way he concludes this statement: the Word was "full of grace and truth."

It would be easy for us to try and pour our own meaning into those words and perhaps not be far off the mark; but it is only as we appreciate their background that we also appreciate their weight. The same pairing of words, but in their Hebrew equivalent, is found in the Old Testament, where they carry the sense of "unfailing love and faithfulness"—God's covenant love and covenant loyalty.

This is seen, for example, in Proverbs: "Let [God's] love and [God's] faithfulness never leave you; bind them around your neck, write them on the tablet of your heart" (Prov. 3:3). In other words, in the midst of our own inescapable sin and failure as we make our way through life, our constant hope is in God's great salvation and his never-failing faithfulness to his covenant promise. We know that we will never find peace with God through what we try to do for him—however well-intentioned—but rather in what he has done for us and covenanted to us in the gospel.

In its Old Testament context that hope rests on a promise that was yet to be fulfilled; but in the New Testament it rests on all that Jesus is and on everything he has done to actually secure redemption for all who trust him. The only way we can be sure that our salvation is real is when we know that the One we trust has both the capacity and the authority to save!

Through the incarnation, Jesus became "God for man and man for God" in order that he might ultimately become "the Savior of world"!

Before a person submits to surgery, one would want to be sure it would be real a surgeon who was going to carry out the operation. How much more, then, if we are going to stake our entire existence in time and eternity on someone's claim to be able to grant us eternal salvation should we want to be sure we can trust him!

STUDY QUESTIONS

The incarnation of the Son of God—Jesus Christ becoming man—is surely one of the greatest mysteries of the Christian faith. In an earlier study, we looked at the "God of the creed." Of all of Christianity's unique teachings, the fact that Jesus Christ is both God and man is what stands out the most, second only, perhaps, to the doctrine of the Trinity. Thus, the Christ of the creed can quite properly be called the God-man of the creed!

Central to this mystery is the virgin birth of Christ. While this doctrine has been mercilessly attacked over the years, it stands as one of the foundational tenets of the Christian faith, as seen in the clause in the creed relating to Christ's unique entrance into this world.

A right understanding of the incarnation is not only spiritually enriching but also necessary. This study will focus on this world-altering truth: God came as one of us.

1. Why was it necessary for Jesus to be born of a virgin? Could Jesus have been conceived any other way?

2. Look up Isaiah 9:6–7. Here Isaiah is referring to the Child prophesied in 7:14. Typical of the prophets, there are elements in Isaiah's prophecy that could have come to pass during the time in which the prophecy was given. However, Isaiah's astonishing words in 9:6–7 show that he is describing the coming of one very different from all other human children.

   a. What four titles does the prophet ascribe to the coming Child?
   b. Why would Isaiah call the coming One "Father" if he is a Child?
   c. What does this passage teach us about God's sovereignty in redemption?
   d. What does this passage teach us about what believers in the Old Testament were taught to hope for?

3. Look up Luke 1:26–38. At the beginning of Luke's gospel, he tells us that he has written these things so that we might "have certainty concerning the things we have been taught" (Luke 1:4).

   a. When Mary questions the angel, why is the angel's reaction different when compared to his reaction to Zechariah's question?
   b. How are the three persons of the Trinity active in these verses?
   c. What does Mary's response to the angel teach us about faith?

4. How is the fact that Christ is born of a virgin central to his death for our sins on the cross?

5. Look up Hebrews 2:14–17. The author of Hebrews is concerned to have his readers understand that Jesus truly became human.

   a. Why would the author of Hebrews want to underscore that Jesus did not come to save angels but "Abraham's descendants"?
   b. What reason does the author give for Jesus' becoming like us? How is this related to Jesus' priesthood?

6. What does Christ being born of a virgin teach us about God's character? How should we live in light of this?

"He Descended into Hell"

There is nothing more central to the Christian message than the cross of Christ. The cross is there in the shadows of the Old Testament. It explodes to the fore in the New Testament, dominating the landscape of the Gospel records. And from the very first sermon preached by Peter on the Day of Pentecost it becomes the hallmark of authentic apostolic ministry. As Paul tells the church in Corinth: "For I resolved to know nothing while I was with you except Jesus Christ and him crucified" (1 Cor. 2:2).

Paradoxically, as church history unfolds in the post-apostolic era, it is the cross that is chosen as the emblem of the Christian faith. In an age when death by crucifixion was still commonplace and the very shape of the cross was enough to send a chill down anyone's spine, the church opted, not for a dove, or an image of the empty tomb, but for the cross to be its "corporate logo." That, perhaps more than anything, is an indicator not only of the cross's significance, but also of its centrality to all that the gospel says.

We see the scale of this significance reflected in the way that the Apostles' Creed skips immediately from confessing the incarnation of Christ to confessing his death upon the cross:

He suffered under Pontius Pilate,
was crucified, died, and was buried;
he descended into hell.

Without so much as the blink of an eye, the architects of the creed gloss over 33 years of Jesus' life on earth, including the three years of his earthly ministry, almost as though these were of no consequence! In so doing they signal the cross as being the defining moment of salvation history and therefore also the keynote of the good news of redemption that they, and we, preach to the world.

That said, we cannot help but wonder at what seems like an unusual choice of words in this particular clause: "He descended into hell." These words are all the more intriguing when we realize that this third line of the triplet was a much later addition to the creed—most likely in the latter part of the fourth century A.D. Not surprisingly, it has sparked no small measure of controversy and debate as to its precise meaning.

Some have argued that the phrase simply signifies Jesus' burial; but that has little merit since it would represent a redundancy of language given the previous clause. Others have argued cogently on the basis of the Greek form of the word for "hell"—"Hades"—that it speaks of Jesus' descent into the realm of the dead for the period between his death and resurrection. This view is argued by a shining galaxy of theologians and preachers and cannot be dismissed lightly. But the problem with that interpretation is that it does not reflect the weight and balance of the biblical exposition of the cross and all that it accomplished. So, given the economy of words employed in the creed, it seems odd to include a statement that reflects something of a mere footnote in the biblical account and its explanation.

It seems more sensible to follow John Calvin (as he in turn followed expositors of the creed before him) and see the inclusion of these words in the Creed as a summary of the two clauses about the death of Christ that precede them. So on the one hand "he descended into hell" sums up the full horror of what is stated almost in a matter-of-fact way in the previous lines; but on the other hand it provides us with the key to seeing all that the cross accomplished for God's people.

Nowhere is the saving significance of Calvary more dramatically expressed than in the words of John the Baptist as Jesus began his earthly ministry. Pointing the crowds to Jesus John says, "Behold, the Lamb of God who takes away the sin of the world" (John 1:29). Indeed, it bears noting that, in a way that is reflected in the emphasis of the creed, John the Evangelist skips from confessing the incarnation of Christ to proclaiming his death! On these two great truths the message of the gospel hangs. Three things are worth highlighting in relation to what the two Johns say as a means of explicating what is said in the creed about the death of Christ.

The Innocent Suffering in the Place of the Guilty

John the Baptist's ministry as the forerunner of the Christ was geared to exposing human sin and guilt and the need for both pardon and cleansing. The limitation of John's ministry was the fact that while he could expose this need, he could do nothing to deal with it. So, when pressed by a delegation from the Jewish authorities in Jerusalem to say who he was, John responded by saying: "I am not the Christ" (John 1:20). Indeed, he systematically denied that he was to be identified with any of the messianic figures bound up with the hope of salvation in the Old Testament. His only message was that people should be looking to the one "who comes after me" (John 1:19–28).

However, when Jesus appeared among the crowds, without any prompting or collusion between himself and John, John declared, "Behold the Lamb!" In language that spoke unmistakably of death, the Evangelist uses the testimony of the Baptist to introduce the ministry of Jesus at its inception by pointing to its climax and conclusion. In other words, both Johns are saying that the entire purpose of Jesus' coming was to do for guilty sinners what they could not do for themselves—die to take their sin away!

By introducing Jesus in this way, John was not only pointing to the fact that he was destined to die, but also explaining in advance the significance of his death: it would be death as a sacrifice. His language is drawn unmistakably from the world of Old Testament ceremonial practice in which an innocent and unblemished creature (that did not deserve to die) was taken and ritually slaughtered in the place of guilty sinners. God was willing to accept—albeit in symbolic fashion—the death of the innocent in order to preserve the life of the guilty. In that sense what John refers to here is more than merely the language of some arcane ritual; rather, it is the language of divine justice. On the one hand it speaks of death as the just consequence of sin. To the ears of our present generation, that sounds harsh, but that is only because today's generation has little or no appreciation of the seriousness of sin. But when we realize that sin is in its very essence a defiance of the authority of God as Lord of the Universe and a disruption of the entire equilibrium of the universe he has made, then it makes perfect sense that grand treason on such a scale demands the ultimate sanction. The God of the Bible is the Lord of Righteousness whose justice is not to be mocked.

The glory of the gospel is that this very same God has instituted a judicial measure by which sin and guilt can be transferred to a third party so that the guilty individual can be pardoned—the entire Old Testament system of sacrifices is built around this fact. God wanted it ingrained into the very psyche of his people that he was simultaneously the Judge of all the Earth and the Savior of the World—without any contradiction between the two.

The question for any Jew, and indeed for any serious reader of the Old Testament, was, "Where, when, and how does the symbol become reality?" God makes it clear repeatedly in the Hebrew Bible that the blood of bulls and goats can never actually atone for the sins of men and women, boys and girls because there is no equivalence between animals and human beings. But even if God had sanctioned the use of *human* sacrifice as a means of making atonement for human sin, such a sacrifice could be no more than the life of one individual for that of one other. It could not atone for the sins of the entire human race. So where is the fulfillment the Bible promises? The answer can only be found in one Person and one place: Jesus the God-man providing the only sacrifice with the capacity to atone as one for many, and the cross of Calvary as the place where that supreme transaction is made.

The judicial element of that transaction is highlighted by Jesus' trial before Pilate. In what in so many ways seems a complete travesty of justice and the ultimate blemish on the judicial system of the Roman Empire, a drama of infinitely deeper significance was unfolding. We have a breathtaking hint of it in the words of Caiaphas the High Priest when he told the Sanhedrin, "It is better for you that one man should die for the people than that the whole nation perish" (John 11:50). Then we see it plainly, as Calvin points out, in the fact that the two charges on which Jesus is convicted before the court of Pilate are treason and blasphemy—the very crimes of which the entire human race is guilty before the court of heaven. The proceedings of the court then climax in what becomes a living allegory in what happens to Barabbas—the criminal convicted of insurrection and murder—when he is released in order that the innocent Jesus might die. The justice being transacted that day as Jesus "suffered under Pontius Pilate" was the justice of God himself. The innocent suffered so that the guilty might go free.

The Blessed One Cursed That the Cursed Might Be Blessed

If it was true that Jesus' trial before Pilate indicated that there was more going on that day than met the eye, then the manner of Jesus' death made that even more clear.

Many people (preachers included) are inclined to look at the fact that Christ died on a cross merely from the perspective of its being a hideous form of the death penalty. If that is all there was to it, then actor and director Mel Gibson was entirely justified in portraying the crucifixion as he did in his film *The Passion of the Christ*. More than that, the British atheist who once got into trouble for saying that by the standard of crucifixions generally Jesus got off pretty lightly, was actually right. The physical torment of crucifixion was undeniably horrendous, but other evil empires throughout history have found even more hideous ways to extinguish human life. So physical suffering alone cannot be the sum total of the anguish Jesus went through that day.

The real anguish of the cross can only be understood against the Old Testament backdrop to all that was taking place. In particular, the fact that God had said, "anyone who is hung on a tree is under God's curse" (Deut. 21:23). That statement probably needs a little unpacking for it to make sense to twenty-first century Western minds. In the first place it should be borne in mind that "hanging" in the ancient Near East meant impalement and not suspension by a rope. So for Jesus to be impaled on a Roman gibbet, meant that this sobering anathema settled on him like a cloud—to the horror of those who loved him and the delight of those who wanted him dead. And in the second place, the idea of cursing in the Old Testament was not some primitive version of what is practiced by witch doctors or Voodoo practitioners today, but rather the judicial element of God's holy covenant. While on the one hand God promises blessing to all who believe the promises of his covenant and submit to its stipulations, on the other hand he warns of cursing for all who spurn his overtures of covenant grace and who refuse to bow to his rule. If the essence of blessing is happiness and harmony as the expression of divine favor, then the essence of cursing is unhappiness and chaos as the expression of divine displeasure.

So, when Jesus was put to death *on a cross* that Friday morning, to all the Jews who were watching, he was seen as accursed. And it wasn't just that there was chaos, confusion, and disorder all around in the scene at Golgotha, but that there was the smell of divine displeasure filling the air. It was a scene made all the more incongruous because the one on the cross exposed to God's curse was the very one of whom the Father had said just three years previously, "This is my Son, whom I love; with him I am well pleased" (Matt. 3:17). But the greatest of all disruptions that day came not in the turmoil that surrounded Jesus, but in the disruption of body and spirit that brought his earthly life to an end—the disintegration that is the supreme anathema of death.

It falls to the apostle Paul to explain the sheer bewilderment of this scene when he tells the Galatians: "Christ redeems us from the curse of the law by becoming a curse for us, for it is written: 'Cursed is everyone who is hung on a tree'" (Gal. 3:13). The Blessed One is cursed so that those who deserve cursing will be blessed!

The Supreme Judge Facing the Final Judgment

It is only when we put these pieces of jigsaw into place as we try to understand what the cross meant that we then appreciate the final clause in the creed's statement about Christ's passion. What could otherwise be seen as something bland

and, though tragic, still somewhat innocuous, is in fact utterly extraordinary.

"He descended into hell" is the starkest and yet most accurate way of summing up what happened on the cross that there is. The Blessed One who, for all eternity had known nothing but the highest heaven of intimacy with God, on the cross plumbed the deepest depths of the anguish of hell in order to secure salvation for all his people. The intensity of what that meant is distilled into the words that pierced the darkness when Jesus cried out, "My God, my God, why have you forsaken me?" (Matt. 27:46).

There was a magnitude to the events played out that day in the drama of Calvary that had eternal proportions. This was nothing less than the drama of the Day of Judgment being played out in human history to show where sin ultimately leads. Christ's cry of abandonment is the preview of the final and eternal alienation of hell: permanent separation from God.

His cry stands as a sobering warning to all who think that keeping God at a distance in this life is a choice worth making. But at the same time it is proof of God's promise to save all those who dare to put their hope and trust in his grace and mercy. God has not only made a promise, but has fulfilled his own requirements by satisfying the demands of his perfect justice to the full, so that he can justly throw open the floodgates of his love for all who believe in his Son.

The cross means that God is able to save with a clean conscience! In this great act is nothing less than the one who will one day be the Judge of all mankind taking the full force of his own final judgment so that sinners might be spared.

"He descended into hell" may be the most controversial clause in the Apostles' Creed, but when seen this way, it becomes the most glorious, because it speaks most eloquently about the justice and grace of God's salvation!

STUDY QUESTIONS

This phrase is probably the most controversial of the entire creed. As noted in the discussion above, it was probably an addition of the late fourth century. However, as we also saw, the phrase highlights the death of Christ in the place of sinners. Coming as this phrase does right after the confession of Jesus' virgin birth, it is wise to remember that his incarnation was unto atonement. Jesus became man to die in the place of his people.

1. Look up 1 Corinthians 1:18–25. Paul is writing to a place that, at the time, was second only to Athens as a center of learning and commerce. But he tells the people of this church that he wants them focused only on the cross.

   a. Paul draws many contrasts here, particularly between "the wisdom of the cross" and the wisdom of "this age." What does this distinction mean?
   b. Why is the cross a stumbling block to Jews? Why is it foolishness to Greeks?
   c. Paul asks a string of rhetorical questions in verse 20. What point is he driving home?
   d. Paul quotes Isaiah 29:14 in verse 19. Why would Paul use this quote from the Old Testament here?
   e. Paul concludes his reasoning in verse 25. What does this verse teach us about God's character in relation to the cross of Christ?

2. Look up Hebrews 10:1–4. The author is drawing our attention to the temporary and external conditions of the sacrificial system of the Old Covenant.

   a. How is the law a "shadow of the good things to come"? What point is the author trying to make by stating the matter like this?

b. List some specific ways in which the Old Testament sacrifices pointed forward to an aspect or aspects of Christ's work.

c. Why would the blood of bulls and goats be unable to take away sin? How does the atonement relate to the incarnation, given this statement?

3. The phrase "he descended into hell" summarizes the prior two clauses of the Creed. How was Jesus' suffering and death on the cross a "descent into hell?"

4. How does God's grace relate to his justice, given the reality of Christ's substitutionary suffering and death? Is there a contradiction between grace and justice?

Jesus Christ: Risen, Ascended, and Enthroned

We began the last chapter by saying, "There is nothing more central to the Christian message than the cross of Christ." That is indeed the case, but it is a statement that needs to be qualified. Just as the cross on which Jesus died literally towered above the landscape of Golgotha, so too it towers above the landscape of the Gospel record and the explication of the gospel message that runs through Scripture. But it does not stand in isolation. Repeatedly we are made to see that the cross only has saving significance in conjunction with three other events.

The creed reflects this in the next clause that speaks of Christ as not only being crucified but as one who "on the third day rose again from the dead . . . ascended into heaven, and is seated at the right hand of God the Father Almighty." The crucifixion is inextricably bound up with the resurrection, ascension, and enthronement of Christ in his work of salvation. Take any one of those four elements out of the equation and the whole structure of redemption collapses. If there was no resurrection, then the atonement is redundant. If there is no ascension, redeemed humanity is abandoned to a sin-cursed world. If there is no enthronement, the Savior lacks the authority to save.

When Jesus asked the Father to glorify him with the glory that was his with the Father before the world began (John 17:1–5), it was this entire sequence of events that he had in mind as the steps that were necessary for that prayer to be answered. As the cross represented the nadir of his humiliation in the place and for the sake of sinners, so the heavenly session secured for him and for them the restoration of the glory God intended.

The wording of the creed at this point embeds this four-dimensional event in our understanding of redemption and reminds us of our need as Christians to seek to plumb its depths. So, having already considered the cross at some length, let us think more briefly about the resurrection, ascension, and enthronement of Christ.

Risen

The Bible's definitive statement about the resurrection is found in 1 Corinthians 15. It is the chapter that begins with Paul identifying those elements of the gospel that are "of first importance" (15:3)—tamper with any of these and we destroy the hope of salvation. Paul refers explicitly to the death, burial, and resurrection of Jesus (15:3–4), and then implicitly to his ascension/enthronement in his post-ascension appearance to Paul on the Damascus Road (15:8). He speaks of all of these as historical events that occurred "according to the Scriptures" but which in turn form the basis of salvation past, present, and future.

It is fascinating to note that as Paul begins to tease out the implications of these events, he dwells not on the cross (despite having said at the start of this letter that he preaches nothing but "Christ and him crucified') but on the resurrection. The immediate reason for this is in part the fact that there were some in the Corinthian church who were denying the possibility of resurrection (15:12). The apostle obviously needed to address that problem at a local level; but the amount of space and detail he devotes to his answer indicates that there is far more at stake than the Corinthians could ever imagine.

Paul sets out in the first place to establish the historicity of Christ's resurrection, citing the multiplicity of witnesses who saw, heard, and touched Jesus during the forty days of post-resurrection appearances (15:4–8), and states that the proclamation of this fact formed the centerpiece of the message the Corinthians had first believed (15:11). He then goes on to challenge the claim that resurrection does not happen. His reasoning could not be more forceful: "If Christ has not been raised, our preaching is useless and so is your faith" (15:14). The resurrection was not an invention of the early Christian community, but a fact of history.

Of all the Gospel writers, Luke devotes the most space to the account of the resurrection and the many public appearances Jesus made in the forty days that followed. As we move into Acts—the second volume of Luke's historical record—we cannot help but notice that the importance of the resurrection continues to feature prominently. It is there at the heart of every major sermon or discourse recorded in Acts and was clearly a vital component of the gospel message as it spread. However, of even greater interest is the fact that the resurrection becomes a key element in the court proceedings that crop up again and again in Acts as the apostles are put on trial, first before the Jewish and then the Roman authorities. Given the legal context of proceedings, the factuality of the resurrection claims are open to cross-examination all the way from the Sanhedrin in Jerusalem to the Supreme Court of Caesar in Rome. If the story of the resurrection had been a myth, it would not have been difficult to produce the bones

63

of Jesus to prove it, or dismantle the testimony of those who claimed it to be true.

Paul builds on this historical foundation by spelling out its implications for salvation. He states that Christ was raised as "the firstfruits of those who have fallen asleep" (15:20). In other words, he is the part-for-whole guarantee of the future bodily resurrection of all who put their faith in him. A salvation that is merely spiritual—in terms of both present and future experience—would be a salvation that is sub-human. For resurrection to be complete, it must involve the resurrection of the body for believers when Christ returns, and that can only happen because Christ himself rose physically from the dead.

Throughout history, the opponents of the Christian faith have targeted the resurrection in particular in their efforts to discredit and destroy the gospel, but they have failed. This most extraordinary event in history is the guarantee of hope in the face of eternity. It seals all that Jesus accomplished on Calvary and allows Paul to taunt death and the grave about their powerlessness (15:55). The resurrection is firmly embedded in the creed because it lies at the very heart of redemption history.

Ascended

The next decisive moment in Jesus' journey from humiliation to glory is his ascension. Luke records the eyewitness testimony of the event as seen by the eleven disciples who were present. In a way it is tempting to skip straight from Easter Sunday to Ascension Thursday in our reflections on the exaltation of Christ, but to do so would be to miss at least one other important detail: the fact that Jesus' resurrection body is the same, but different.

It is the same as his pre-resurrection body in that it is physical; but it is different in that it is not immediately recognizable. Mary, the disciples on the road to Emmaus, and others who saw Jesus after he emerged from the tomb did not immediately realize that it was Jesus. That was not merely because they were so overwhelmed by the reality of his death that their brains were overriding what they were seeing, but that there was actually something qualitatively different about him. On the one hand he was visible, tangible, and capable of eating and drinking; on the other hand he could appear and disappear without the use of doors or windows. He still bore the marks of nails, thorns, and a spear, but nevertheless was different.

Jesus himself hints at what that difference entailed when he said to Mary Magdalene, "Do not hold on to me, for I have not yet returned to the Father" (John 20:17). In other words, although he had already been exalted through resurrection, that exaltation was not yet complete. Paul fills in the blanks for us in chapter 15 of 1 Corinthians when he describes the resurrection body of the last Adam, Christ, as being a "spiritual body" (15:42–49). What he means by that is not that Jesus was some kind of specter; rather, he had a body suited to the realm of the Spirit—that is, heaven.

The body with which Jesus emerged from the tomb was a body that belonged to the world to come. It was absolutely right and proper for him to reveal himself in that body for that forty-day period to confirm that he was indeed alive and to allay the fears and suspicions of his followers; but it would have been entirely inappropriate for him to remain in this present world in a body that belongs to a future world. That was the body/new humanity he took into heaven when he ascended.

Even here we need to stop and question ourselves as to how we understand what we mean by that. The creed's wording, "he ascended into heaven," echoes what the angels said to the astonished disciples who were gazing into the space into which they had just seen Jesus disappear (Acts 1:10–11). But what does "into heaven" mean? J. I. Packer makes some pithy observations on this in his comments on the creed in

I Want to be a Christian.[1] He rightly points to the cloud in which Jesus was enveloped as being the key to understanding all that was going on. Far from being merely an unexpected fog that engulfed Jesus at that moment, this was nothing less than the glory-cloud that in the Old Testament is synonymous with the presence of God. That is entirely consonant with the primary meaning of "heaven" in Scripture: the "endless, self-sustaining life of God"—perfection. But there is more to it. If the secondary sense in which "heaven" is used in the Bible is "men and angels sharing the life of God," as Packer says, then Jesus' taking his resurrected body into that cloud was his restoring our humanity to where it really belongs.

Movie-goers are well used to the "coming soon" previews of films that are yet to be released. The resurrected Christ is the ultimate sneak peek for what is yet to come for those who have faith in him. He is, as my friend Rev. Ian Hamilton, minister of Cambridge Presbyterian Church in Cambridge, England, so often says, "the prototypical man." The ascended Christ takes us beyond what Adam was in Eden to what Adam was meant to become had he fulfilled his duty to our race. So our hope of salvation extends as far as heaven itself, where we in Christ will perfectly share the life of God for all eternity.

The ascension is far more than just the next step in Jesus' journey home: it is nothing less than the guarantee of home-coming for all who put their trust in him.

Enthroned

There is, of course, one other clause in this section of the creed: the affirmation that the risen, ascended Jesus is at this moment "sitting on the right hand of God the Father Almighty." He is enthroned in heaven. He is reigning on high.

1. J. I. Packer, *I Want to Be a Christian* (Eastbourne, UK: Kingsway Publications, 1977), 53–57.

One of the most amazing little details in Luke's account of the earliest days of the New Testament church in the book of Acts is the fact that a mere seven days after Jesus' ascension, Peter declares that Jesus is "exalted to the right hand of God" (Acts 2:33) as the supreme fulfillment of all that God had promised to and through King David. That same note is sounded again in Hebrews when the author says of Jesus that, after the ordeal of the cross, he "sat down at the right hand of the throne of God" (Heb. 12:2). He is exercising God's executive rule over the entire world and universe. In the language of Paul,

> Therefore God exalted him to the highest place and gave him the name that is above every name, that at the name of Jesus every knee should bow, in heaven and on earth and under the earth, and confess that Jesus Christ is Lord, to the glory of God the Father. (Phil. 2:9–11)

The one whose appearance and true identity were obscured and marred almost beyond recognition through his incarnation and then his crucifixion, is now exalted to his rightful place as Savior-King of the world. He is there directing all things for his people's good (Rom. 8:28), providing for their needs and protecting them from evil. But even greater still is the fact that his enthronement gives warrant to our faith. He is the one alone who has authority to save. Those who look to him will never be put to shame.

There is one other little detail in all this that cannot be overlooked. It is the fact that Christ's enthronement means our enthronement too. Paul tells the Christians in Ephesus, "And God has raised us up with Christ and seated us with him in the heavenly realms in Christ Jesus, in order that in the coming ages he might show the incomparable riches of his grace" (Eph. 2:6–7). Christ restores in us our true dignity and authority as human beings. He equips us for his service in this world. He prepares us for the perfection of the life to come in the future world he has promised for his children.

We said at the start that the cross is indeed central to the message of the gospel, but it does not stand alone. It is only as we follow Jesus through the cross to the empty tomb, the cloud of glory, and the throne of heaven that we see the full picture the gospel paints and the ultimate hope that is found in Christ alone.

STUDY QUESTIONS

Many people think only of Christ's crucifixion or resurrection. But, as the creed teaches, Jesus has risen, ascended, and is seated at the Father's right hand, reigning in all his glory. These four elements—crucifixion, resurrection, ascension, and enthronement—are all necessary, or, as has been noted, "the whole structure of redemption collapses." We serve the risen and reigning King of Glory!

1. Look up 1 Corinthians 15:1–11. Paul is detailing here the historicity of the crucifixion, resurrection, ascension, and enthronement.

   a. Why does Paul say this is "of first importance"? What does he mean by "he received this"?
   b. Why is Paul so concerned that his readers understand that all of these events happened "according to the Scriptures"?
   c. What does the phrase "last of all, he appeared to me" teach us about Paul's view of the office of apostle? What are the qualifications for an apostle that Paul lists in this passage?
   d. Paul treats all of these events as historical and absolutely true. How does knowing that is so help us in

speaking to unbelievers? What significance does the historicity of these four events—crucifixion, resurrection, ascension, and enthronement—have for our evangelism and our faith?

2. Look up Acts 1:9–11. Jesus is taken up into heaven in a cloud, ascending to his Father after appearing to the disciples.

   a. In Acts 2:1–4, we read of the outpouring of the Holy Spirit. How does the ascension of Christ relate to the outpouring of the Holy Spirit? What Old Testament connections does Peter draw between the work of Christ and the outpouring of the Holy Spirit?

   b. What is the significance of the cloud in Jesus' ascension? What is the preeminent Old Testament passage that mentions God's people being led by a cloud? What else does the cloud imagery of the Old Testament teach us about Christ?

   c. How does knowing that Jesus ascended in a new, resurrected body affect how we look at our lives? What does it teach us about how we should look at our own bodies or the bodies of others? How does this help us minister to a culture obsessed with body image?

3. Look up Ephesians 2:4–7. Paul is recounting to the Ephesians the glory of their complete salvation by God.

   a. How is it possible that though we still live here, we are enthroned with Christ, as Paul teaches?

   b. Man was originally created with dominion over creation (cf. Gen 1:26–28). Because of the fall, that dominion was retained but tainted. How does Christ's ascension restore—and make better—the original authority of mankind? How does the ascension affect how we care for creation, as the renewed humanity in Christ?

   c. Question 26 of the Westminster Shorter Catechism asks, "How doth Christ execute the office of a king?" The answer comes: "Christ executeth the office of a king, in subduing us to himself, in ruling and defending us, and in restraining and conquering all his and our enemies." As an enthroned King, Christ is subduing our enemies. How should that change our outreach? How should it affect how we deal with trials and tribulations and difficulties?

d. Look up Psalm 110:1. How does Jesus fulfill this (cf. Hebrews 1:13)? How are evangelism and outreach the work of "footstool building" for King Jesus?

e. Jesus tells us that his kingdom is not of this world (cf. John 18:36). Given this and the current atmosphere of religious bigotry in radical Islam, how should we as disciples of Christ advance his kingdom? What methods does Jesus authorize?

When Jesus Comes Again

T he New Testament refers some three hundred times to the return of Christ, so this event is not something we can easily ignore or sideline in our understanding of the faith. Yet, it is an aspect of the Bible's teaching that has been largely overlooked in recent times—at least in many Reformed churches. There may well be several reasons behind this oversight in the current teaching patterns of the church.

On the one hand it may be a reaction against the obsession with eschatology and *parousia* theology which dominated the post-war and Cold War eras of the twentieth century. The general uncertainty of those times, with national emotions still raw from the memory of two world wars and the very real fear of a nuclear holocaust , meant that apocalyptic literature in the Bible seemed all too relevant. Authors like Hal Lindsay had a field day playing fast and loose with imaginative exegesis of every end-of-the-age prophecy from Daniel to Revelation. But, when it turned out that Henry Kissinger was not the False Prophet after all and the European Common Market did not become the final catalyst for the Rapture, credibility of these doomsayers began to wane. That in turn has fed into a growing cynicism, fuelled more recently by the multi-million dollar *Left Behind* industry.

71

On the other hand, the movement away from interest in the Second Advent has also been fostered by the apathy that has emerged out of growing global prosperity. The sense of our having "heaven on earth" with a relatively comfortable standard of living, and of war becoming an increasingly regionalized phenomenon, has steered interest away from the age to come. (One can only watch with interest to see what will happen if we end up in a prolonged global recession and an escalation of international conflicts.)

Regardless of where public interest—both Christian and secular—may currently be leaning, we cannot ignore the weight and frequency of biblical references to this theme. Indeed, going back to where we left off in our last chapter, the Christ who is resurrected, ascended, and enthroned is the Christ of whom the angels said, "This same Jesus, who has been taken from you into heaven, will come back in the same way you have seen him go into heaven" (Acts 1:11). So, as we follow the creed at this point, it takes us from the resurrection and exaltation of Jesus to his return in glory. Having acknowledged his exalted status at "the right hand of God the Father Almighty," its next clause goes on to say, "from thence he shall come to judge the living and the dead."

It would be impossible to do justice to all that is contained in that brief statement, but let me try to tease out three major implications of this strand of theology that come to light in one of Christ's own references to his return: "The Son of Man is going to come in his Father's glory with his angels and then he will reward each person according to what he has done" (Matt. 16:27).

The Direction of History

We cannot help but be struck by the context in which Jesus spoke these words. At first sight they seem out of place coming as they do after a statement about the prospect of his sufferings and the cost of discipleship. The problem, however, is that we tend to atomize this passage. It is one of the richest segments in the Gospels. It begins with Peter's confession of Jesus as the Christ and goes on to record Christ's response to that confession as he declares his avowed intent to build the church on the apostolic "rock," guaranteeing its survival against every scheme of hell to the contrary. It reaffirms the necessity of Christ's death and resurrection in securing that future for his people, and it declares the radical cost of discipleship for those who would become followers of Jesus. Does that mean, then, that Jesus' statement about his *parousia*, and the eternal kingdom it will usher in, must sit awkwardly like a "widow and orphan" at the bottom of the page in all of this? The answer to that has to be a resounding "No!"

The issues and exchanges recorded in this chapter of Scripture are of such enormous importance that we cannot simply dissect them into their component parts. The central element of the chapter—Peter's confession—marks such a watershed, not only in the chapter, or even the Gospels, but in all of Scripture. It is clear that what follows must have the effect of reconfiguring the way God's people think. What they had only glimpsed and guessed at in the shadows of Old Testament revelation now bursts forth into the full light of day, which in turn makes them look afresh at what they thought they understood already.

So, most significantly, the great Old Testament motif of the "Day of the Lord" begins almost immediately to take on a new complexion. What had been perceived in the days of the prophets as a single day marking the end-point of history—simultaneously being the Day of Judgment on the wicked and deliverance for the righteous—is suddenly seen to be a very different kind of "day." Far from being the final twenty-four hours in the history of planet earth, it is seen to be the final day-age period in God's history of redemption. The judgment that John the Baptist so confidently expected would accompany salvation with the coming of the Christ (Matt. 3:10–13) was actually judgment deferred. (Or, more accurately, judgment that would be conferred on the Christ "now" for the righteous, but which was still future for the wicked.)

So, as Jesus moves seamlessly from cross to resurrection to discipleship to his return to the kingdom that is to come, he is giving his followers a deeper understanding of history. The key link in his chain of reasoning that takes us beyond the Jewish concept of history is when he says, "What good will it be if a man gains the whole world, yet forfeits his soul?" (16:26). He is reflecting the way the human mind instinctively thinks: always in terms of this world—the here and now. We become so taken up with this life that we do not stop to think what lies beyond it. (And even when people do in theory acknowledge that there is a future life in a world to come, they live in practice as though it doesn't really matter.)

Jesus challenges that mindset, making it clear that history has a very definite direction and that we are all caught up in its movement. Just as his own death and resurrection were to be decisive moments in the unfolding of that history, so too would be his return in glory at its close. He is saying in brief in this verse what he will say at much greater length in the Olivet Discourse (Matt. 24:1–51), and what becomes a major theme throughout the remainder of the New Testament right through to its great climax in the book of Revelation: there is one day in the future that colors every other day in between. It is the day of his visible, personal, regal return that will bring history as we know it to its conclusion.

There is nothing academic or esoteric about that fact. Just as all our little journeys in life are colored by the destination to which we are traveling, how much more so is the great journey of life itself. As the single thread of our personal history is woven into the tapestry of unfolding world history, so the direction of both is the same as they take us inexorably towards that day when Jesus comes again. Our confession of the Christ who "will come" is a perpetual reminder of our need to travel through life with a real sense of where it is heading and not just shamble along aimlessly as though this world is all there is to life. Jesus will surely come and we must be ready to meet him.

The World in Eternity

The return of Christ will mark the cut-off point in history. It will be the day when the world as we know it will end and a whole new order will be ushered in. Jesus alludes to this without going into detail as he says that when he comes, "he will reward each person in accordance with what he has done"—using "reward" in the sense of "ushering in the consequences of the choices people make in this life." There are at least two major issues bound up with that, one of which we will deal with in a moment, but here let me focus on the first that relates to the future of the cosmos.

In his call to true discipleship, Jesus has already spoken of the world in its present state. It is a world that is full of attraction, and there is a deeply-rooted human longing to have it in full. Jesus puts a monumental question mark over that yearning by pointing to his return at the end of the age. Even if it were possible for one individual to have his wildest dreams come true—he wins the global lottery and the world is his, for example—all that would count for nothing as he crosses the line between history and eternity. He has gained the whole world; but that is all he has gained!

That may sound like weak logic on Jesus' part. If Faust was willing to sell his soul to the devil for the rewards he was offered, then the even greater reward of "the world" sounds like an infinitely better deal. But, to borrow a title from a James Bond movie, in the eyes of Jesus, "The world is not enough!"

The "reward" he will give to those who have lived and labored only for this world and what it has to offer will be in part that their wish will be granted. They will have their world—and their world will turn to dust in their hands.

Jesus knows what such people do not know: this present world is passing away and will one day come to a dramatic end. It will not just be that the earth we regard as home will be finally destroyed; rather, the entire created order as we know it will be completely dismantled.

It is the apostle Peter who speaks most graphically about the future of creation in its present state in his second letter. There he says, "But the day of the Lord will come like a thief. The heavens [universe] will disappear with a roar; the elements will be destroyed by fire and the earth and everything in it will be laid bare" (2 Peter 3:10). The world as we know it is imperfect. Worse than that, it is a world under divine curse, and it can never be an appropriate and enduring home in which God and his people can enjoy unending communion. So those whose entire life revolves around the here and now are seriously misguided in their outlook on life.

We could well raise issues of man's recklessness at this point—the waste of natural resources, the human factor in climate change, and the like—all of which expose our shared guilt for bad stewardship of the planet— but that would be a distraction. As the race increasingly focuses on its own failures, which have led to our present woes, there is a shared conviction that man-made problems must also have man-made solutions. But the Bible takes us way beyond that. Wastage is only a symptom of what really lies behind these issues: the problem of human sin. It was because of human sin that the creation as a whole was cursed, and it is only when the problem of sin is fully dealt with that the curse will finally be lifted. That problem is beyond our reach to solve. The only credible solution is the one that God himself has provided through his Son. It was through his death and resurrection that the new creation has been ushered in (2 Cor. 5:17), and it will only be when the outworking of his redemption is complete that the new creation will finally replace the old.

That brings us to the positive counterpart in what Peter says about the future of the world: "But in keeping with his promise we are looking forward to a new heaven and a new earth, the home of righteousness" (2 Peter 3:13). The world in its present fallen state will be destroyed, but in its place will come a renovated world and universe—an event that Jesus describes as "the renewal of all things" (Matt. 19:28). This is the world God has planned for eternity, the perfect home Christ is already preparing for his people (John 14:2–3). This is the true "New World" that Jesus will usher in on his return.

The Race and Its Destiny

There is, of course, one final and somber note to sound in relation to this particular doctrine. It is the fact that the prospect of Christ's future coming is bound up with that of final judgment. "He will come to judge both the living and the dead."

It will not be as a helpless babe in a manger, or with his glory veiled behind a humbled humanity, but in the full blaze of his glory, in the glory-clouds of heaven, with the entire host of heaven itself as his entourage. On that day the dead will be raised and every human being who has ever lived will stand before him as the Judge of all the earth. There they will be "rewarded" [judged] for whatever they have done in this life.

For the wicked, who have never acknowledged their sin and never acknowledged God, there will be no escape. Their sins and guilt will finally catch up with them. They will be called to account and be found guilty as charged before the court of heaven. For them are reserved the horrors of eternal death—permanent separation from God and his goodness: what the Bible calls "hell." It is a doctrine so fearsome that we tremble to believe it and need great care and sensitivity as we proclaim it.

For those who in this life have believed the good news and put their faith in Christ alone for their salvation, although they too must stand before that throne of judgment, it will be to hear in court what they have been assured of already: that they have been acquitted. Not because of any righteousness of their own or atonement they could make, but all because of the Lamb who sits in the midst of the throne. The one they face as Judge is the one they have already known as Lord and Savior. He has taken their place, secured their righteousness, paid their penalty, and drawn the sting of death so that for them it is no more.

That day will indeed be the "great" day of the Lord; but it will also be "terrible." The mere thought of it drives home the exhortation of Peter to all who will listen: "Since everything will be destroyed in this way, what kind of people ought you to be? You ought to live holy and godly lives as you look forward to the day of God and speed its coming" (2 Peter 3:11–12). The day of man is nearly over; the day of God is coming and all should live in the light of what it will bring.

The brevity of this little clause in the creed belies its enormity. It should make us think again about the doctrine of the second coming and the place it has in our lives and preaching.

STUDY QUESTIONS

When the popular culture speaks of the "end times," people's imaginations are usually filled with images of empty cars on freeways after "the Rapture," a terrifying (usually Middle Eastern) figure arising as the Antichrist, and other events. However, the return of Christ is not a doctrine meant to enflame our imaginations; rather, it is meant to drive us back to Scripture to think clearly about this central article of the Christian faith. The heart-cry of every Christian should be some of the last words of the Bible: "Amen. Come, Lord Jesus!" (Rev. 22:20).

1. Look up Acts 1:6–8 and Matthew 25:36. In the Acts passage, Jesus is giving his disciples their "marching orders," so to speak. But they are interested (just like us!) in the end times!

    a. What does Jesus' response (v. 7) teach us about speculation concerning the date of Christ's return?
    b. The disciples still had visions of a nationalistic restoration of the glories of Israel. Where does Jesus focus their attention? How should that change our focus as we await the return of Christ?

2. Look up Hebrews 1:1–2. The author of Hebrews is teaching us a lot here about the character of God's Word. But he also teaches us about "these last days."

    a. According to these verses, when did the "last days" begin?
    b. There is a "movement" to God's giving us his Word in history. What was the purpose of God's progressive and historical unfolding of his Word over many thousands of years? What is its central purpose, according to the author of Hebrews here?
    c. What does this verse teach us about the structure of history? Is history "going somewhere"?

3. Look up Matthew 25:31–46. This is an awe-inspiring description of the final judgment and separation of all people.

    a. Nowhere in the Bible do we find any notions of reincarnation, an endless cycle of years, or anything but a linear portrayal of history—in other words, history is going somewhere. According to this passage, what two options await all people? Where else do we see such sharp separations in Matthew's Gospel—i.e., a seeming black and white contrast (righteous and wicked)?

b. Notice that Jesus first separates and then judges, showing that our salvation is all of grace—the rewards come after the separation! Nevertheless, what is surprising about the reaction of the righteous in this passage?

c. What is the nature of the punishment of the wicked in these verses? What is the significance of the fact that the kingdom was "prepared" for the righteous and the punishment is "prepared" for the wicked?

d. The idea of eternal, bodily punishment in hell is an idea that is utterly derided in our culture at large and causes even many Christians to stumble. What are some ways that we can constructively engage people who find this idea troubling? What does this passage teach us about salvation and judgment? How does that help us engage those struggling with the teaching of hell?

I Believe in the Holy Spirit

The stark brevity of the Apostles' Creed's affirmation of the doctrine of the Holy Spirit is enough to give many Christians in today's church apoplexy. To their ears it sounds almost insulting to the third Person of the Trinity after having said so much by comparison about the Father and the Son. But then again, perhaps today's church is not the benchmark of orthodoxy when it comes to this doctrine.

Strange as it may seem, as Sinclair Ferguson has said elsewhere, the last three decades of the history of this doctrine have overturned almost two millennia of consensus of belief on who the Spirit is and what role he is pleased to fulfill.[1] The protests of recent generations of Christians—who have been intoxicated by the post-Azusa Street obsession with signs, wonders, tongues, and prophecy—that the Holy Spirit is the forgotten Person of the godhead are more than a little misguided.

He is, indeed, as former generations would have said, "the quiet Person of the Trinity," but that is not the same as saying he has somehow been sidelined in the church's belief and practice through the centuries. As we trace out what is said

1. See Sinclair B. Ferguson, *The Holy Spirit* (Downers Grove, IL: IVP Academic, 1997).

about him in the Scriptures, we discover that it is actually his pleasure to be self-effacing and to direct attention to the Son and to the Father, gladly putting himself at their disposal. (One cannot help but wonder if there is any correlation between this shift in shared belief about the Spirit and the confusion that emerged generally in the twentieth century over equality of the sexes and the difference between their roles.)

Another major misconception about the Spirit that has spread over the past hundred years is that he is a New Testament phenomenon. Pentecost has become the paradigm for pneumatology. To be sure, it is right to say that the Holy Spirit steps out of the shadows of biblical revelation on the Day of Pentecost; but that is only after a whole gamut of glimpses of him literally from the very start of the Old Testament. For the disciples, Pentecost was in some ways like being aware of "an important person" hovering in the background, working away behind the scenes—the headmaster in school, or the CEO of a big corporation: people are aware of his existence, but have never actually met him. But then he steps out of the shadows into public view and all that changes. That is very much what happens as the Day of Pentecost and the sending of the Spirit mark the final stage in the transition period that took God's unfolding purpose from the era of the Old Covenant to that of the New. When it happened, a whole torrent of teaching—both from the Old Testament and from Christ—would have come flooding back to them as all they had learned about God's Spirit took on fresh depths of meaning when they saw him poured out upon the world. At least six major truths about the Holy Spirit would have crystallized in their minds.

The Spirit of God

For those who think that the Holy Spirit is found only in New Testament history and teaching, it comes as something of a shock to realize that we actually meet him for the first time in the second verse of the Bible. There Moses says, "Now the earth was formless and empty, darkness was over the surface of the deep, and the Spirit of God was hovering over the surface of the waters" (Gen. 1:2).

There is, as exegetes will tell us, the linguistic possibility that the word translated "Spirit" in this verse could mean nothing more than "spiritual energy" or "force," or perhaps be intended as nothing more than an allusion to God's presence. But there are other clues embedded in the text and its context that suggest otherwise, clues that point to his being a Person in his own right.

When God says later on in chapter one of Genesis, "Let us make man in our image" (1:26), we must at least raise an exegetical eyebrow over what lies behind it. Yes, the plural of majesty is indeed a possibility, but as with the whole of God's unfolding revelation there is a sense here that we are to "watch this space" and discover that there is more than meets the eye. This becomes even more apparent in Jesus' bizarre use of language in the Great Commission when he tells the disciples that they are to make disciples of all nations, "baptizing them in the name [singular] of the Father and of the Son and of the Holy Spirit" (Matt. 28:19). It sounds like bad grammar, but it is an exquisite revelation of the being of God.

As later New Testament revelation is given, we discover that the Holy Spirit is a "he" and not an "it," that he can be "grieved" (Eph. 4:30)—only a person can be grieved—and that he along with the Father and the Son is worshipped as God.

Why is this important? Because the Holy Spirit is not merely some power put at our disposal; he is the great third Person of the Trinity before whom we must bow. He is none other than the Spirit of God revealed.

The Spirit of Revelation

The second great fact about the Spirit that began to crystallize for the disciples at Pentecost and in its aftermath was that he had not only revealed himself on that day, but had all along been the one who had been making God known through his Word. Even though in a very special sense Jesus had made God known through the incarnation (John 1:18), it had been the Holy Spirit as the divine Author of Scripture who had been doing so for millennia beforehand.

Much later on, Peter put it this way: "For prophecy never had its origin in the will of man, but men spoke from God as they were carried along by the Holy Spirit" (2 Peter 1:21). This tallies with what Paul had said earlier to Timothy: "All Scripture is God-breathed" (2 Tim. 3:16)—with *theopneustos*, the composite Greek word Paul coined for the occasion carrying an overt allusion to the *pneuma*: the Spirit-breath of God.

In other words, through the ages people had and have been able to meet with God in the pages of Holy Scripture in a way that is real and personal because these are not merely the words of men about God—like every other "holy book"—but rather the words of God about himself.

It is clear from a closer look at the Old Testament that this was not some doctrine that was only coined by the New Testament writers. We see it most clearly where David says, "The Spirit of God spoke through me, his word was on my tongue" (2 Sam. 23:2). In other words, the Bible is nothing less than God speaking by his Spirit in language men can understand.

When we grasp this, we realize that the obsession with the word-gifts of the Spirit that has pervaded the church for over a century is actually a major distraction. The function of tongues, prophecy, words of knowledge, and discernment in New Testament times was to meet the need of a rapidly spreading gospel and rapidly expanding church in a unique period when the fullness of God's Word had not yet been given.

As any parent is dismayed when a child will not let go of the temporary stop-gap present when the real present has been given, so too is God dismayed with his children who do not fully grasp what it means to have a Bible!

The Spirit of Christ

One of the most obvious and yet most overlooked aspects of the Spirit and his work is his role in relation to Christ. A simple glance at a concordance to see how often he is mentioned in the Gospels says it all!

It is by the power of the Holy Spirit that Jesus is conceived in the womb of the Virgin Mary (Luke 1:35). It is the Spirit who descends from heaven visibly in the form of a dove at Jesus' baptism and the inauguration of his public ministry (Luke 3:22). It is the Spirit who both empowers and leads Jesus as he launches out into that ministry from the outset (Luke 4:1). So too the Spirit plays a part in Jesus' death (Heb. 9:14) and exerts his power in Jesus' resurrection (Rom. 1:4). The Holy Spirit is Christ's closest companion in his journey to earth from glory right through to the moment of his ascension.

So post-Pentecost, as the disciples looked back over his life and work with the benefit of hindsight, the words Jesus spoke to them in the upper room—which seemed so enigmatic at the time—began to make perfect sense. When he said, "I will not leave you as orphans, I will come to you" (John 14:18), he was talking about the coming of his Holy Spirit. Calling him "the Counselor" (*parakletos*; John 14:15) was the key. It was a term often used in a legal context to describe the "best friend" a person could bring to stand by and support him in court. So it dawned on the disciples when the Spirit came that the very one who had been Jesus' best friend and sustainer during his earthly life and ministry was to be their best friend and sustainer as well! (The fact that he is also described as "another" Counselor pointed to his being "another of the same kind"—what he would be to them would be qualitatively the same as he had been to Jesus!)

Why does this little detail matter so much? In part because it was as perfect man that Jesus found the Spirit's support so vital. Perfect man was never meant to "go it alone." So, what Adam discovered to his cost when he lost the Spirit's sustenance in the Garden, Christ re-proved and restored through his incarnate life and ministry. But it is even more significant when we stop to think of what is the greatest blessing the Spirit can impart: that of Christ himself!

The Spirit of Salvation

Seminarians studying the doctrine of the Holy Spirit are more often than not surprised by the fact that what is billed as a course about the Holy Spirit actually turns out to be (what seems to them) more about the Christian life. Yet when they look again at the Bible and what it has to say about the Spirit and his work, they realize that this is far and away the most significant element of his work.

This fact is rooted in what Jesus says to Nicodemus: "I tell you the truth, unless a man is born of water and the Spirit, he cannot enter the kingdom of God." (John 3:5). Jesus was making it clear that Nicodemus's most basic problem in life was that he was spiritually dead and that he needed nothing less than to be "born from above" (3:7) in order to truly live.

Left to our own resources and devices, none of us could even begin to grasp either the full depth of our spiritual need, or the fact that God has fully met that need through his Son. Again, Jesus, in the Upper Room discourse, speaks of the work of the Spirit in conversion:

> When he [the Spirit] comes, he will convict the world of guilt
> in regard to sin and righteousness and judgment: in regard

to sin, because men do not believe in me; in regard to righteousness, because I am going to the Father, where you can see me no longer; and in regard to judgment, because the prince of this world now stands condemned. (John 16:8–11)

How is a person persuaded of his or her sin, guilt, and liability before God? Through the Holy Spirit's work in him or her. As the Spirit shines the light of God's Word into the darkness of sinners' souls he shows them that they are under judgment. Of course, his work does not stop at that point. It is the same Spirit working through the same Word that causes people not only to see their need, but also to see Christ as their only hope and Savior, and so he brings them to be "born again, not of perishable seed, but of imperishable, through the living and enduring word of God" (1 Peter 1:23).

Having brought them to new birth the Spirit does not then abandon them. As the sanctifying Spirit, he renews and remakes them from the inside out in the image of Christ—a work that he continues until they are taken into glory. Thus, just as the Holy Spirit was with and upon the Lord Jesus from his conception until his return to heaven, so too he is with all God's children from their new birth until he takes them home. He is the Spirit of salvation!

The Spirit of the Church

Given all that has been said so far, it comes as no surprise to discover that the Holy Spirit is also the Spirit of the church. Nowhere is this seen more dramatically than in the opening chapter of Revelation and the words of salutation and blessing to the church:

Grace and peace to you from him who is, and who was, and who is to come, and from the seven spirits [or, sevenfold Spirit] before his throne, and from Jesus Christ, who is the faithful witness, the firstborn from the dead, and the ruler of the kings of the earth. (Rev. 1:4–5)

The existence and spiritual health, well-being, and effectiveness of the church of Christ on earth are all inseparably bound up with the Holy Spirit's presence and work in her midst. The church is by definition "charismatic"!

The dimensions of the Spirit's presence and work among God's people are woven through almost everything that is said about the church throughout the New Testament. The Spirit produces the fruit of godliness in our lives—not only as individuals, but also together as God's new community (Gal. 5:22–23). He enables God's diverse people to live together in unity in fellowship with Christ (Eph. 4:3). He assures us of true faith and salvation (Rom. 8:16) and is the one who enables us to pray (Rom. 8:26). He provides the gifts and graces we need for service in God's kingdom (1 Cor. 12:1–11).

So it follows, as Paul says to the Ephesians, that the church's greatest need on earth is to "be filled with the Spirit"—or, more literally, "keep on being filled with the Spirit" (Eph. 5:18).

The Spirit of Witness

Jesus spoke one final and all-important word to the disciples about the Spirit and his work that is crucial to our understanding. It is found in what Jesus says as he prepares them for his ascension: "You will receive power when the Holy Spirit comes on you; and you will be my witnesses in Jerusalem, and in all Judea and Samaria, and to the ends of the earth" (Acts 1:8). Many Christians instinctively want to cut that verse in half. They are quite content with the idea of the Holy Spirit coming as the one who imparts power (even if it is only the apostles Jesus has in view, as is, strictly speaking, the case). But Jesus does not break the verse this way. The power the Spirit gives—first to the apostles, but also to those who receive

88

the apostolic testimony—is to enable them to bear witness to the Christ! For these disciples, weak and fearful as they were, the Holy Spirit would clothe with the power and boldness they needed to proclaim Christ to the nations.

So too for all who are disciples of Christ. The whole thrust of the Spirit's work in us is that we might be empowered and emboldened to proclaim Jesus to the world as the Savior of the world. This is the litmus test of the Spirit's presence in the church. It is not primarily a matter of "the gifts" or of the style of worship, but this: do we bear witness to our Savior before a world that is lost without him?

STUDY QUESTIONS

The twentieth and early twenty-first centuries are unprecedented for interest in the Holy Spirit. As noted above, he is "the quiet Person of the Trinity." The creed treats the Spirit's person and work briefly, but the brevity should not betray the depth! The Holy Spirit's activity in the Scriptures is like watching TV in black and white versus watching it in color: once you see his work throughout the Bible, you'll never read it the same way again.

1. Look up 2 Peter 1:19–21 and 2 Samuel 23:2. Here, we have at least two explicit references to the "inspiring" activity of the Holy Spirit in the production of the Scriptures.

   a. If the Holy Spirit inspires ordinary people to write the Word of God, how can the Bible still be said to be without error? What guarantees inerrancy in the Bible as the Spirit gives the Word?

   b. Peter's statements are considerably strong concerning the Spirit-inspired nature of the Bible. In what other places does the Bible teach that the Scriptures were inspired by God, particularly the Holy Spirit?

c. How does the Christian view of the inspiration of the Scriptures by the Holy Spirit differ from other religious groups who claim to have "a holy book"? How do some of these other groups try to counterfeit the truth in their claims to have holy scriptures?

2. Look up Revelation 1:4–5. Here we see a reference to the Trinity and a very specific and unique reference to the Holy Spirit.

a. What is the significance of calling the Holy Spirit "the seven spirits" or the "sevenfold Spirit"? What does the number seven signify?

b. What does this passage in Revelation teach us about the Spirit's work in the church? How does he reveal God to the people of God?

3. Look up John 15:26 and 16:7–11. Here Jesus gives us focused teaching on the work of the Holy Spirit.

a. What, according to John 15:26, is the Holy Spirit's chief work in this age? How should this inform how we think about the so-called "miraculous gifts" that people claim?

b. What three things does Jesus say the Spirit will do in John 16:7–11? Why would it be to the disciples' advantage (and ours!) that Jesus should go away?

c. If the Spirit's work is to focus us on Christ, how does that inform our reading of the Bible? How should we think about the Scriptures the Spirit inspired?

4. Look up 1 Corinthians 2:14–16. Paul tells us here that there is a basic difference between all human beings: those who have the Spirit and those who don't.

a. What does Paul mean by "the natural person"? How does this verse affect how you view evangelism?

90

b. Who is the "spiritual person"? What does Paul mean in this verse (v. 15)?

c. Given this basic difference between all people that Paul outlines here, what do these verses teach us about how we should pray for those who do not believe the gospel? What do these verses teach us about our privileges as Spirit-indwelt believers?

Glorious Body, Radiant Bride

F ew things are more precious to Christ and yet more neglected by his people than the church and what the Bible has to say about it. The church is his body and bride. He shed his blood for her salvation. Yet churches and Christians pay scant attention to what the church is and why it matters. In recent times especially, evangelical Christians have become more interested in "personal salvation" than salvation in its grander form as set forth in the gospel—Christ's coming to "save a people for himself."

It is striking therefore, that the creed confesses what it means to believe in "the church" before it goes on to speak of individual conversion and Christian experience. The creed states, "I believe in the holy catholic church; the communion of saints"—eloquently capturing the way in which the corporate and the individual elements of salvation come together in this very visible and tangible way in the shared life of God's new community. At one and the same time it expresses not only the importance attached to the church by God, but also how we as Christians are to appreciate our place in it.

This is a note that desperately needs to be re-sounded today for a number of reasons—largely because of the way that post-Enlightenment individualism has conditioned us to think. We instinctively think in terms of the individual's being the supreme reference point for everything else, instead of realizing that our identity as individuals has roots that run far deeper and wider than anything we could ever be in ourselves. At the most basic level, personal identity is shaped and governed by the families into which we were born. So too in an even more wonderful way our Christian identity is shaped and governed by the spiritual family into which we have been reborn, and especially by the one who is both its Lord and Savior, Jesus Christ.

Sadly, this is something that many if not most Christians have lost sight of today. In broad evangelicalism, Christians are so obsessed with their personal tastes and needs that "church" has become little more than the spiritual equivalent of the supermarket—you take your pick as to which chain of stores best suits your tastes and your pocketbook. But the same is also true in a different way among those of a Reformed persuasion. Too often those who have come to a Reformed understanding of Scripture have embraced a truncated form of Calvinism— one that is concerned only with soteriology and not with that full-orbed understanding that leads to a biblical worldview, and, more importantly, a biblically balanced doctrine of the church. The early church fathers, whose fingerprints are found all over this ancient creedal document, were Calvinists before their time! They saw the church in all her glory and sought to express that in this next clause of the creed.

They were doing nothing more than to echo what the apostle Paul was saying to the church in Corinth—a church that was also suffering from spiritually skewed vision in relation to this doctrine. They too were more concerned with individual spiritual identity than with what they were corporately in Christ. So Paul speaks at considerable length, expounding the definitive statement about who and what we are as Christians: "You are the body of Christ" (12:27). In other words, he wanted the Corinthians to realize that understanding what we are as Christians can never be separated from what it means to belong to the church.

If we use that statement, and the larger context of the chapter in which it occurs and of the letter as a whole, then it will give us a useful template to explore what lies behind this clause in the creed. Three things come to light as being of central importance in the doctrine of the church.

The Church Is Holy

Paul raises the issue of church from the very outset in his letter to Corinth. In his opening greeting, he addresses his readers as "the church of God in Corinth" (1 Cor. 1:2). Even though he is addressing a congregation that was brimming over with difficult individuals, he begins by reminding them of their shared identity. They are not "the church of Corinth," but "the church of God in Corinth." And, just in case the full weight of what that means did not sink in immediately, he goes on to say that they are also "sanctified in Christ Jesus and called to be holy." Belonging to God and being holy go hand in hand.

What does that mean in practice? At the most basic level it means that the church is set apart by God and for God. It belongs to him and exists for his glory. So even though we so often speak of the churches to which we belong as being "our" church, in reality they belong to God. That means that it is not up to us to set our own agendas for something that is not ours. We must always seek and serve the agenda set by God himself. To appreciate that the church is "holy" means first and foremost to realize that God is her Lord.

If that is true, then it must have a major impact on how those who belong to the church actually live—hence the statement about their being "sanctified in Christ Jesus and called to be holy." What these people were in principle was to be worked out in practice in their daily lives. Their sanctification was, on the one hand, to use Professor John Murray's expression, "definitive"; but at the same time it was also to be "progressive." True holiness is not merely a state; it is an ongoing transformation in which the people of God grow to be more like God both in their individual and corporate lives.

That had to be a staggering thought for the congregation in Corinth, which in so many ways could not have been less like God in view of the personal conduct of many of its members and the sheer disunity that had become its hallmark. But Paul knew that, and he was in no sense seeking to crush these people with the shame of their failure. Rather, he was reminding them that their calling in Christ was to be different, and, as he will bring out later, the reason they have been given the Spirit of holiness is so that they may actually become more holy in how they live (1 Cor. 6:19–20). Could it be true of the professing church of our day that her relative ineffectiveness in her work and witness—despite large numbers—is her scant concern for holy living? Robert Murray McCheyne could not have been more right when he famously wrote in a letter to a missionary friend, "It is not so much great talents that God blesses, but great likeness to Jesus. A holy minister [or Christian, or church] is an awful weapon in the hand of God."[1]

There is one more thought that links in with this aspect of what Paul has to say about holiness and the church: accountability. In his opening remarks, Paul speaks of our need to be "blameless on that day [the day of Christ's return]" and that this blamelessness is ours through Christ alone (1 Cor. 1:8). The implication behind what Paul was saying here is that among those who professed to be Christians in Corinth there were those who were Christian in name, but not in reality.

---

1. This letter can be found in Andrew A. Bonar, *Memoir and Remains of Robert Murray McCheyne* (London: Banner of Truth, 1966), 282, but the quote itself is available in a number of places online.

The visible church will always be mixed. As the Westminster Divines so helpfully put it, "The purest churches under heaven are subject both to mixture and error" (WCF 25.5). But for all who are part of the church visible, there is an accountability that goes hand in hand with holiness.

This is implied in what Paul says later on in 1 Corinthians about the children and unconverted spouses of believers being "holy" (1 Cor. 7:14). This does not mean that they are automatically regenerate, but it does mean that they have a special standing in God's sight. On the one hand they are uniquely privileged to live in such intimate communion with the gospel, but at the same time they have a responsibility for how they respond to it that is greater than those who live outside the church community. In the same way as the liability of Chorazin, Bethsaida, and Capernaum will be greater on the day of judgment than that of Sodom, Tyre, and Sidon (Matt. 11:20–24), so it will be for all who are part of the holy community visibly, but not spiritually.

The only way a person can be sure that he or she will indeed be "blameless on that day" is by looking to Christ alone for standing before God. The holiness that is the mark of the church is a holiness that is found in Jesus.

The Church Is Catholic

When the creed says the church is "catholic" many people instinctively read that as meaning "Roman Catholic." But that is not at all what is in view. The term "catholic" is used in the creed to speak of the church in its totality, or what is sometimes called "the church universal." It picks up on what Jesus said in that defining moment of his earthly ministry at Caesarea Philippi: "I will build my church and the gates of Hades will not overcome it" (Matt. 16:18). Jesus did not say, "I will build my churches," but rather, "my church." There is ultimately but one church of Christ that is found in many places and in many different expressions throughout the world, across history and linked into eternity. So even though individual congregations each have their own flavor and distinctives, they are all ultimately part of the one church universal. The church cuts across all denominational and cultural boundaries and leads us finally to what the church will be in her perfected state in the glory of the world to come.

Grasping the catholicity of the church has enormous implications for how individual churches see themselves and how they relate to other churches. No church is allowed to be parochial in its outlook. We are part of something that is infinitely bigger than anything we could ever be in ourselves, so our horizons of church life must always be reaching out to that larger body to which we belong. It means too that we must guard ourselves against the "not one of us mentality" for which Jesus chided his disciples so severely (Mark 9:38). We can become so blinkered by the particular concerns and distinctives of our own congregations and denominations that we lose sight of the "sheep that are not of this fold" that belong to Jesus every bit as much as we do (John 10:16).

It is tempting to restrict our understanding of the church's catholicity to what it is in macrocosm, but it has a dimension that relates to what the church is in microcosm as well. Just as unity within diversity characterizes the church in its universal expression, so too those same features should define every local congregation. If we go back to Corinth and what Paul says to the church there, we see that he reminds the Corinthians not only that they all together are the body of Christ [in that place], but also that "each one of you is a part of it" (1 Cor. 12:27).

Those words carried a particular resonance for that particular church. Paul has already spoken of the party spirit which was disrupting the fellowship of the church and which had become the talking point in the gossip columns of the Christian world of that day. It was not just that the church community in Corinth reflected the amazing breadth and diversity of the local community—from a former synagogue ruler to converted prostitutes—but that this newly-formed church family was becoming fragmented. People were being excluded because they did not fit into particular groupings in the church.

Paul could not have been more forceful in the way he addressed this situation. He speaks in graphic terms of a muti-lated body and uses that as a reflection of what the spiritual body in Corinth had become (1 Cor. 12:14–28). The Corinthian church's failure to embrace one another in Christ was a viola-tion of Christ himself.

The challenge to be catholic Christians runs to the very heart of what it means to be truly Christian, and ironically it can often be those Christians and churches to which we are closest geographically that we find it hardest to embrace. If we face the prospect of sharing heaven with them for eternity, then perhaps we need to think again about cultivating fellow-ship with them on earth.

The Church Is a Communion

The third thing we learn from what Paul says about the church is that it is ultimately a communion. We see it in the extraordinary way in which Paul speaks interchangeably about Christ and his church: "The body is a unit, though it is made up of many parts; and though all its parts are many, they form one body. So it is with Christ (1 Cor. 12:12)." In other words, if we are joined to Christ in saving union, then we are simul-taneously joined to all his blood-bought children in the full breadth of that union expressed in the communion of saints. All that we are and have as his people we share together with all his people. As we share the same baptism of the Spirit and "drink" of one Spirit, so we share the same spiritual DNA and enjoy one and the same salvation.

The full depth of what that means brings us back to what went wrong with our race at the very beginning and to God's original intentions for humanity. As man was made uniquely for union and communion with God, so his union and communion with his fellow human beings was contingent on that primary relationship being intact. When relationship with God was broken through the fall, the immediate second casualty was the relationship between Adam and his wife, and thereafter, with his whole family. The glory of the gospel is that in salvation God reverses the damage of the fall on both planes.

We rightly emphasize the importance of communion with Christ as lying at the heart of healthy Christian living; but we cannot do that honestly without putting equal stress on cultivating the communion we enjoy together as his people. It reflects the fact that we are joined together in the same family of God.

The problem Paul was addressing in Corinth was the fact that the church in that city was behaving like the ultimate dysfunctional family and in so doing was damaging the credibility of the gospel. So he comes back again and again to what it means for them corporately as much as individually to be "in Christ Jesus."

It can hardly slip our notice that in the prayer Jesus offered on the eve of his arrest and crucifixion, he prayed at length and repeatedly that his followers "may be one ... so that the world might believe that you [the Father] have sent me" (John 17:20–24). There is no greater visible proof that the gospel is good news than the fact that it really does rescue and transform relationships—cutting across barriers of race, class, and culture in a way that shocks the watching world. Jesus only ever identified one mark of a true church: "By this all men will know that you are my disciples: if you love one another" (John 13:35). The earthly communion of saints is God's great billboard that advertises the power and glory of the gospel.

Almost forty years ago, Michael Griffiths wrote a book about the church, the title of which described it as *Cinderella with Amnesia*[2]—the princess who had forgotten who she was. There is a certain timelessness about that description because it seems that so many Christians and churches have simply forgotten who we are and what we have become in Christ. We are his glorious body and one day will become his radiant bride!

STUDY QUESTIONS

An alarming trend in modern Christianity (in the West at least) is the wholesale questioning of the usefulness of the local church. With books being published that call for believers to disavow churches, the need for a right understanding of the church is urgent indeed. So important was the church to the framers of the Apostles' Creed that they made the church a fundamental article of the Christian faith. This study will focus on the biblical aspects of the church.

1. Look up Ephesians 4:1–16. Paul gives a description here of the nature of the body of Christ, the church.

   a. What is Paul's purpose of mentioning "one Lord, one faith, one baptism" (vv. 4–6)?
   b. Paul says that Christ has given gifts to his church in the form of officers. What does this teach us about how we should think about those who teach and preach God's Word in our churches?

---

2. Michael Griffiths, *Cinderella with Amnesia: A Restatement in Contemporary Terms of the Biblical Doctrine of the Church* (Downers Grove, IL: InterVarsity Press, 1975).

   c. What are some of the purposes of the instruction from teachers in the church, according to Paul?

   d. What does this passage teach about our gifts as believers? What are we to do with our gifts?

2. Look up Ephesians 5:25–33. In this passage, Paul compares Christ and his church to a husband and wife.

   a. How does Christ treat his bride, the church? What does that teach Christian husbands and wives?

   b. If marriage is Paul's chosen metaphor, then what does that teach us about our bond as believers to Christ? How can we communicate the truths of this passage in a culture saturated with divorce and broken marriages?

   c. According to verse 26, what does Christ do for us? How does he accomplish this?

   d. What do these verses teach us about the importance of the church? Where can you love God's people more in your week in, week out experience as a church member?

3. The creed talks about the "catholic church." As pointed out above, this does not refer to the Roman Catholic church, but to the church universal. How can we be better "catholic Christians"? How can you reach out to those in other churches to show the bond of Christ that you share with other believers?

4. Since the church is a communion of saints, how does that change how you look at those sitting next to you every week in worship? Have you reflected on the truth that you will spend eternity with these people? How then should we live now as believers together?

Salvation in Shorthand

Our journey through the creed has taken us from the heights of glory, contemplating God in his triune majesty, through to the new community Christ is building in the church. But as we have been confessing these great truths, we might by this stage be forgiven for wondering, "Where do I fit into all of this?" This is, of course, the burning question of personal salvation and what it entails. Without individual salvation there is no fellowship with God and no place in his church. And, given the greatness of God and the beauty of his church, we know almost instinctively that "salvation" must be a wonderful thing. So, as we hold our breath for the words that will confess this great salvation, we might well be taken aback to hear just one line: "I believe in the forgiveness of sins."

Why could it not be "I believe in the new birth," or "I believe in the life of holiness," or an even more comprehensive summary of these and the many other dimensions of the salvation promised in the gospel? Does it not feel more than a little lame to reduce such a grand concept to these few words and to express it in such negative terms?

The answer lies quite simply in the fact that without the forgiveness of sins there can be no salvation—no knowledge of God, no new birth, no place in his family, no holiness, and no heaven. Human sin and guilt combine to exclude us from every other blessing that might be ours in salvation. Until they are dealt with, we are left outside.

There is perhaps a sense in which people in every circumstance can identify with that—even those who have never given the Christian gospel a second thought. No matter how good a person's life may be, it is the common experience of every human being to be unsettled by a guilty conscience. From Lady MacBeth's dramatic, "Out! Out! Damned spot!" to the ordinary man or woman haunted by the past, guilt is the running sore of the soul. There is an ingrained sense of failure at the heart of the human condition, and so the quest for atonement becomes a common thread that is woven through life. It provides the storyline for countless books and movies. It is everyday reality for every honest member of our race. So those who framed the wording of the creed once more proved their perceptiveness when they used this striking single line as shorthand for "personal salvation"!

In many ways they were simply picking up on the way Paul condensed the essence of salvation to a very similar phrase in Colossians. Summing up all that is involved in it, he says: "For he [the Father] has rescued us from the dominion of darkness and brought us into the kingdom of the Son he loves, in whom we have redemption," which is "the forgiveness of sins" (Col. 1:13–14).

Despite all that is wrapped up in God's saving work as mentioned in this verse, and all the apostle has already mentioned in the preceding verses—faith, love, hope, fruitful living, a growing knowledge of God and spiritual power, endurance, patience, and joyful thankfulness—it all hinges on one thing alone: "the forgiveness of sins."

The stark simplicity of it all is salutary because almost every generation of professing Christians manages to lose sight of this core truth at some point or other. It is well worth our while to explore this theme a little further in light of what Paul says in these verses and tease out its implications for our understanding of the gospel.

Why Forgiveness of Sins Matters

If we were to ask the average person what he or she thought was necessary to make someone a Christian, it is not hard to imagine what responses would be given. They would be very much the kind of things Paul mentions in his prayer of thanksgiving for these Christians in Colosse. A Christian is a person who knows God, who possesses spiritual wisdom and understanding, lives a life characterized by good works, and possesses qualities of strength and endurance, even when the going gets tough. There is no arguing with the fact that all these traits and qualities are indeed the mark of a person who has found true and saving faith; but in themselves they do not make a person a Christian, because none of them on their own, or even together, can bring a person into a relationship with God that is real and that can grow.

The fundamental problem we all share is that before we can even begin to cultivate any of these elements of being in fellowship with God, we need to reckon on the fact that we are actually cut off from him because of sin. So salvation can never merely be building up something that is already there, because the simple fact is that there is nothing there to start with. Indeed, the opposite is the case. We do not even start from a point of spiritual neutrality in relation to God; we are actually under his wrath and condemnation.

The quest for salvation can never be reduced to a quest for knowledge or a futile attempt to somehow please God, because such actions—and everything like them—have failed before they have even begun. The problem with all such human attempts to find our way back into fellowship with God is that they do not take seriously what God says about himself in his Word—in particular, the fact that he is both just and holy. His holiness means that he cannot tolerate sin in any shape or form in his presence—he is "of purer eyes than to look upon evil and tolerate wrong" (Hab. 1:13; my translation). And his justice means that he is obliged to deal with it.

It is an indictment on recent generations that we have become so inured to wrongdoing in society that we are no longer shocked: the threshold of moral tolerance has risen to the point where pretty much anything goes. The effect of such "tolerance" is that when evil and wrongdoing—even in their simplest forms—go unchallenged, very quickly they start to ruin all with which they come in contact.

That can never be the case with God. He remains consistently and implacably opposed to all sin, because even the smallest and seemingly most insignificant of sins are the beginnings of rot in his world. Indeed, we see it most clearly when we go back to that time when there was no sin in his world—the time when the entire creation was perfect in every way. In that context, God's warning to Adam that a seemingly trivial infringement of eating forbidden fruit from a single tree would result in death might seem rather extreme (Gen. 2:17); but when we see how quickly the destructive power of sin begins to spread, we realize it is not extreme in the least.

Every good gardener will take drastic action at the slightest sign of weeds in his beloved plot of land; how much more, then, will the divine Gardener do what is necessary to prevent his Paradise-Garden from being ruined forever. Death—separation of man from God—was the necessary consequence of the fall, or else God would have ceased to be God. The only way a reversal was possible was if the root of this separation was dealt with, thus allowing sin to be forgiven. It is for that reason that forgiveness of sin is the absolute bedrock of a salvation that is real. And it is for that reason that the Protestant Reformation was forged on the anvil of forgiveness—the rediscovery of justification by grace alone, through faith alone, in Christ alone. Everything else in salvation hangs on that single thread. It is only when a person is pardoned, cleansed, and restored to fellowship with God through faith in Jesus Christ that "all spiritual blessings in the heavenly realms" that Paul describes in his letter to the Ephesians can be ours. The idea of "sins forgiven" may sound simple, but it could not be more crucial.

What Forgiveness of Sins Costs

Going back for a moment to what Paul says in Colossians, we see that he uses two other words in this passage to describe what salvation is: "rescue" and "redemption." Both words point to God's answer to man's attempts to find deliverance from a guilty conscience by his own effort. History is full of examples of how man tries to make his atonement for himself, from the idea of appeasement of the gods so common from earliest times, right through to the recent book-turned-movie *Atonement*, in which the central character literally writes a book in order to rewrite her past and expunge her sense of guilt and shame. All of these efforts involve a cost (and often the theory is "the costlier the better"), but they never seem enough to actually make amends for the offence that has been caused. God's answer brings the whole concept of cost in salvation to an altogether different level, and the two words Paul uses here bear that out.

The "rescue" Paul has in view is "from the dominion of darkness," that realm in which we all live in this fallen world: a realm that is dominated by evil, even in the very best it has to offer. The language of rescue conjures up images of those who go on missions into places of great danger in order to save others already trapped there. Whether it be venturing into a raging storm, a burning building, or whatever, there is a cost to getting people out. We should not underestimate the cost to God in simply entering our world in the Person of his Son, Jesus Christ. The Light of the World was coming into a world of darkness; the Creator was taking the flesh of the creature. The price tag on that seemingly simple step was enormous in terms of the humiliation it involved. Yet it was a price that Jesus did not balk at paying.

There was, however, more to it. The rescue mission Jesus embarked on would also involve "redemption." Such language was commonplace in biblical times and immediately brought to mind scenes from the world of slavery—of people deprived of rights and freedoms and yet who so often longed for liberty. In particular, this language refers to the cost to purchase freedom. For those who were in bondage, a high price had to be paid if they were to be set free. Throughout the Bible the language of slavery is used to describe people whose lives are still controlled by sin. It is not only graphic imagery, it is also chillingly accurate, because a slave does not control his or her own life; slaves are controlled by a master. So it is in every human being: by nature we are under the control of an alien power from which we cannot break free by ourselves. We cannot afford the price to purchase freedom.

Given the ugliness of the world into which this language takes us, there is an exquisite beauty in that one word that speaks of liberation—a beauty intensified by the cost bound up with it. It is a word that brings us ultimately to the cross where the supreme price was paid to set God's people free.

Where Forgiveness of Sins Is Found

In one sense we have already answered the question of where this forgiveness we so much need can be found; but before we jump to say the words, let us look again at how Paul expresses it in Colossians. Speaking of Jesus as the "Son he [the Father] loves," Paul says, "in whom we have redemption, the forgiveness of sins" (Col. 1:14). Although indeed it is through the cross that our redemption is purchased and forgiveness secured as children of God, it is not the cross in isolation that does so. It is the cross of Christ and it is, as Paul says elsewhere, through "Jesus Christ and him crucified" (1 Cor. 2:2) that we receive redemption and forgiveness.

Paul's choice of words in this verse is anything but insignificant. Let me illustrate it this way. There have been a few times in my life when I have been privileged to be taken to places that are normally off-limits for the average citizen. One in particular stands out. It was the opportunity to be taken onboard *HMS Hermes*—at that time the pride of the British Navy—when she was moored in Manhattan Docks. The aircraft carrier was not long back from the Falklands War in the South Atlantic and was still under a high level of security, yet I was taken all over the vessel. Why? Because I had a friend who was an officer in her crew. Because of him I was given access to places from which I would otherwise have been excluded.

So it is in salvation. As we have said already, we are all by nature excluded from the most important place of all because of our sin. We are barred from the presence of God. Like Adam, we are banished from the Garden. Like Cain, we are doomed to be "restless wanderers on the face of the earth" (Gen. 4:14). But that is not true of Jesus. It is not just because as the Son of God he has known nothing but intimate communion with God through all eternity, but that as true man who rendered perfect obedience on behalf of his people he has regained the right of access into that holy of holies for all who believe. And, of course, central to his obedience is the fact that that obedience was "unto death—even death on a cross" (Phil. 2:8).

So in the fullest possible sense—indeed a sense that was not possible prior to his incarnation and sacrificial death on the cross—Jesus alone has right of access to the richest and deepest communion with God. And if we know him as our Friend, then in him that right is ours as well! As John so beautifully puts it at the beginning of his Gospel: "Yet to all who received him, to those who believed in his name, to them he gave the right to become children of God" (John 1:12). What we have no right to in ourselves, we receive the right to through Jesus Christ—a right he could only confer after his death on Calvary.

It is, of course, for that reason that hymn writers from Toplady to Townend have never tired—and will never tire—of writing hymns about the cross! Far from being a morbid fascination with a gruesome form of death, a celebration of the cross is a celebration of the most glorious achievement the world has ever seen. That climactic moment in the personal history of Jesus Christ is the defining moment in salvation history. It is the key to sins forgiven and, because of that, the key to salvation in all its fullness.

Therein lies the logic of the creed. It tells us about God—who he is, what he is like, and all he has done through Christ—and then it tells us about ourselves and what it means to receive his salvation. It could not be clearer: to have fellowship with God, we need forgiveness, and apart from Christ and his cross that never could be ours.

Perhaps nowhere do we see this truth expressed more poetically and with such passion than in the words of David in his great penitential psalm, where he says: "Blessed is he whose transgressions are forgiven, whose sins are covered. Blessed is the man whose sin the Lord does not count against him and in whose spirit there is no deceit" (Ps. 32:1–2). This is the blessing of salvation in its fullest measure.

STUDY QUESTIONS

As we have noted again and again in our study of the creed, the brevity with which it treats certain topics should not be taken to mean that such things are unimportant. The line "I believe in the forgiveness of sins" may be one of the shortest in the creed, but it is certainly one of the most important. Without the forgiveness of sins, there is no good news. We have just focused on the corporate aspect of the Christian life; in this study, we will look at what this means for us as individuals.

1. Look up Psalm 51:1–6. This psalm is an eloquent confession of sin—and assurance of pardon from a gracious God!

   a. What does David say about himself in these verses? What do they teach us about our character as human beings?
   b. What does David say about God in these verses? What is he like?
   c. What do these verses teach us about the nature of sin? Can God merely write it off and forget about it?
   d. David goes on in this psalm to ask God to purge and clean him. How is this fulfilled in Christ? Where do we see this taught in the New Testament?

2. Look up Mark 10:32–34. Jesus foretells his death and resurrection in this passage.

   a. What does this passage teach us about the nature of Christ's death? Was it an accidental happening?
   b. What does Christ's death teach us about the cost of forgiveness? Is salvation "totally free"? If so, for whom and why?
   c. This portion of Scripture ends on a hopeful note, yet not many of Jesus' disciples understood what he was saying. Why was that? Do we fully understand what the forgiveness of our sins cost? Why or why not?

3. In the Old Testament, forgiveness only came at the cost of blood, sacrifice, and substitution (cf. Lev. 1–5). How did the sacrifices of the book of Leviticus teach the Old Covenant

people of God about the work of the coming Messiah? What do they teach us today about God, sin, and ourselves?

4. Look up Matthew 18:21–35. Jesus tells a parable about an unforgiving servant.

   a. The debt the servant owed the owner was enormous— roughly equivalent of a lifetime's salary in today's numbers. What does this teach us about our sin?

   b. What does the servant's response to the owner's grace teach us about our response to God's forgiveness? Why is forgiveness so hard for us?

   c. In verse 35, Jesus gives us the point of the parable. Is he teaching that our salvation is dependent on our forgiveness of others? What does he mean?

   d. Where in your life do you need to practice forgiveness? How does knowing that God forgave all your sins for the sake of Christ change how you look at any wrongs committed against you?

Resurrection and Restoration

As we come to the last of our studies in the Apostles' Creed, we cannot help but be struck by the way the creed ends: I believe "in the resurrection of the dead and the life everlasting." Given the brevity of the preceding statement on the forgiveness of sins, there is something in us that wants to hear more about the "here and now" of the life of faith; but instead we're taken directly to the "there and then."

Whatever frustration we might feel over what seem like major gaps in the creed regarding what we need to know about God and salvation, we must remember that it is a creed and not a full-blown confession of faith. Its purpose is to provide the key contours and coordinates of the Bible's teaching and what it means to be a Christian. As we have seen already in our journey through its clauses, the creed's brevity should not be mistaken for paucity. Each clause is in a very real sense the distilled essence of a truth that is much broader and deeper than it appears on the surface. And the way in which each clause is related to all the others provides the framework we need for understanding the heart of authentic Christianity.

So, having been told how the Christian life begins in pardon and reconciliation, we are now told where it finally leads: here is the great destiny toward which salvation is taking us. The very fact that the creed makes this seemingly giant leap from faith's beginning to its end speaks for itself of the weight of significance attached to each. Although Christians are so often inclined to look back to where it all began in their own experience—the point of their conversion—it is vital that they never lose sight of where it will all end. If we take our eyes off of where we are going, we will almost certainly lose our way and lose our confidence as the journey unfolds. Or, to put it another way, if we see the Christian faith merely as something that will improve the quality of life in this present world, then we are guaranteed to be disappointed. As Paul so rightly tells the Corinthians, "If only for this life we have hope in Christ, we are to be pitied more than all men" (1 Cor. 15:19).

This important truth recurs repeatedly throughout the Scriptures and especially in the writings of Paul. It is to Paul's own testimony in his letter to the Philippians that we now turn to help us see more clearly why this matters so much. There Paul makes it clear that for him and for God's people generally, the Christian life is governed by one thing above all others: "I want to know Christ and the power of his resurrection and the fellowship of sharing in his sufferings, becoming like him in his death, and so, somehow, to attain to the resurrection from the dead" (Phil. 3:10–11). This then crystallizes in his final statement at the end of that chapter: "But our citizenship is in heaven. And we eagerly await a Savior from there, the Lord Jesus Christ, who, by the power that enables him to bring everything under his control, will transform our lowly bodies so that they will be like his glorious body" (Phil. 3:20–21).

As we draw these studies to a close, let us try and unpack what Paul means by this and see how it well expresses what is summarized in the final clause of the creed.

A Permanent Home

Paul speaks about "citizenship"—where people really belong. He uses that language deliberately because his audience in Philippi belonged to a Roman colony and prized the Roman citizenship which went with it. The sense of pride and security that was very much part of being citizens of Rome is no different from the many expressions of citizenship found throughout the ages and throughout the world. A passport is a wonderful thing; it identifies you as being part of a larger whole, and carries the sense of permanence and belonging. Paul says that for him and every true Christian, "home" is ultimately heaven. Here in this world—often quite literally—he was a restless traveler; but there in the world to come he would be forever settled.

The United States Immigration authorities have a wonderful way of reminding those who come from other countries to work or study in America that they are only here temporarily. The authorities stamp the immigrants' documents with the words "Resident Alien," and that says it all. "You can live here, work here, enjoy what is on offer in this country; but you don't ultimately belong here!" How gloriously true this is for those who are Christians, whose true citizenship is in heaven.

Paul puts it eloquently earlier on in Philippians in one of his best-known sayings: "For me, to live is Christ and to die is gain" (Phil. 1:21). Although Paul already knew Christ and the salvation found in him in this life, the very best of what that could mean in this world would be eclipsed by its fullness in the world to come.

For Paul and for all Christians, that means there will always be a holy discontent with our experience of the life of faith in this present world. Having tasted of the powers and perfection of the age to come, we can never be fully satisfied until we enter permanently into that world. Like those who have dined at the Ritz only to return to their local MacDonalds and never quite enjoy it as they used to, so with those who have come to know and love the Lord Jesus Christ. What we enjoy already will always be affected by the sense of anticipation of what is yet to come.

Paul picks up that theme when he speaks so candidly of his own experience in the third chapter of Philippians. Having written of the perfection to which he looks forward (Phil. 3:11), he goes on to say, "Not that I have already obtained all this, or have already been made perfect, but I press on to take hold of that for which Christ Jesus took hold of me" (Phil. 3:12). He knows the tension between the "already" and the "not yet" of Christian experience, and that is very much what the creed wants us to grasp. The creed sums up the Christian life in terms of what we already enjoy—forgiveness—and what is still in the future—life everlasting in its fullest sense.

Christianity is ultimately an otherworldly religion: it sets our horizons for life firmly in the future, in the whole new world that Jesus is preparing for his people. So Christians live their lives here echoing the words of the old Negro Spiritual: "This world is not my home, I'm just a-passing through." This must give us all pause for thought—especially in an age that is obsessed with the present. As the author of Hebrews puts it: "For here we do not have an enduring city; but we are looking forward to the city which is to come" (Heb. 13:14). There we will have a home that is permanent.

A Perfect Existence

It is hugely important to appreciate what kind of future existence Paul is anticipating, because too many Christians have had misguided notions about heaven and what it will be like. The most widespread idea is of some kind of ethereal existence in the form of disembodied spirits. Such a view of the future life is at best unnatural and at worst subhuman, since our bodies are an essential part of our humanness. This view carries overtones of the Gnostic heresies that did such damage to the church in the late first and early second centuries A.D.

Paul's hope for the future is bound up inextricably with the hope of a resurrected body. He has alluded to it already when he speaks of somehow attaining to the resurrection of the dead (Phil. 3:11), but at the end of the chapter he spells it out categorically, saying that when Jesus returns, he "will transform our lowly bodies so that they will be like his glorious body" (Phil. 3:21). The key to understanding what lies behind this is seen in the previous verse where he says of Jesus that he has the "power that enables him to bring everything under his control" (Phil. 3:20). In other words, the resurrection of the bodies of individual believers who have died will be part of the renewal of all things when Jesus comes again.

It is crucial to see those two things side by side and in relation to one another. There is no use having a perfect body for an existence in an imperfect world. Just as a pristine Lamborghini sports car could never be "at home" in a ghetto, neither would a perfect resurrected body be at home in a world still spoiled by sin. The apostle looks forward to a totally transformed existence in a totally transformed environment—a perfect life in a perfect place.

It is that double reality that the creed captures so well as it runs these two clauses together: "the resurrection of the body and the life everlasting." Notice that it does not merely speak of "life everlasting," but "*the* life everlasting." Immortality in itself is no guarantee of joy and blessing. The devil and his demons and all who die rejecting God will also have a never-ending existence; but it will be one that is the opposite of perfect.

The clue to understanding the kind of perfection envisaged in these words is Christ himself. It was he who proclaimed himself to be "the resurrection and the life" (John 11:25) and he of whom Paul says, "in him all things hold together" (Col. 1:17). Or, even more explicitly, Paul writes to the Corinthians,

117

"Therefore, if anyone is in Christ, New Creation!" (2 Cor. 5:17; my literal translation). The essence of God's new creation will be a world and universe in which Christ is consciously acknowledged as the one upon whom all things depend and to whose lordship all will submit.

At one level all this has major implications for how we prepare ourselves for death and face it when it finally comes. That is true for each of us personally: we need to see that death is not the end and that Christ is our only hope for the future. It must serve also as a comfort to those who mourn the death of Christian loved ones. There are few more precious words in a funeral service than those spoken during the committal of the body to the ground: it is laid to rest "in the sure and certain hope of the resurrection of the body." And historically it has controlled the way that Christians have treated the mortal remains of the deceased with dignity and respect—because those same mortal remains will one day be raised to immortality.

At an even greater level, however, these truths about the future must shape our expectations of life itself. Even though we share a longing for a life that is better than what we can ever know it to be in our present existence, we will neither abandon ourselves to cynicism and despair, nor detach ourselves from the present in mystical escapism. Rather, we will wait patiently for the day of Christ's appearing, looking forward to all that it will usher in. We will cling to the certainty that there is indeed such a thing as a perfect existence—but it can only come in heaven.

A Powerful Incentive

It would be all too easy to turn these teachings into the kind of spiritual escapism that we have just mentioned—allowing them to become a spiritual version of the virtual reality existence found in the cyber world of such online fantasy games as *Second Life*. (That has been the case throughout church history with the bizarre array of sects and communes that have tried to manufacture some kind of heaven on earth.) But for Paul these truths have radical relevance for the present.

Far from using this strand of Christian teaching as an excuse for running away from the pressures and demands of life in this world, he sees them as the means for facing those demands with courage and determination. So he rounds off his train of thought in this section with these words: "Therefore, my brothers . . . that is how you should stand firm in the Lord, dear friends!" (Phil. 4:1).

Paul's outlook on life stands in stark contrast to those who have no genuine hope of a future life. Indeed, he speaks earlier of those who live only for themselves and for this present age, saying, "Their destiny is destruction, their god is their stomach, and their glory is in their shame. Their mind is on earthly things" (Phil. 3:19). For them, life without God becomes a misery in the present long before it leads to endless agony in the future.

Paul's readers might well have been tempted to dismiss what he was saying here as being the ultimate spiritual con: claiming something that is impossible to prove or guarantee. But that is not what Paul is doing. His hope for what God has promised for the future rests firmly on what God has done in the past. He "presses on to lay hold of" the future only because Christ has already taken hold of him for that future in his past (Phil. 3:12). And for Paul that was not merely his personal conversion experience on the road to Damascus, but, rather, the once-for-all accomplishment of redemption through the death and resurrection of Jesus. Everything God has promised for eternity has its foundation in history in all he has done through sending his Son as the Savior of the world.

That grand certainty of the past undergirds our great confidence for the future, both of which converge and find their focus in Christ and all he has come to do.

Several years ago the pop star and international fund-raiser Bob Geldof published his autobiography under the title *Is That It?*[1] As far as Geldof was concerned, he had "done it all" in terms of what this life could possibly offer—from self-indulgence to public-spirited self-sacrifice—yet he was left with that empty feeling that life really doesn't amount to much. Sadly, that epithet is the story of many lives: lived to the full by this world's standards, yet hollow and empty. The glory of the Christian gospel is that this does not have to be the case. The full depth and scope of that gospel—embodied as it is in the Apostles' Creed—begins in the heights of glory with God and it ends in even greater glory with man restored to perfect fellowship with God in Christ.

There is no greater truth this world has ever seen and no greater message it could ever hear!

STUDY QUESTIONS

We come now to our last study. The creed has taken us from the glories of the triune God to the day-to-day affairs of our lives as Christians. Appropriately, the creed closes with a clause about our future hope of a resurrection body and life eternal with God. These are some of the most wonderful and sublime truths to contemplate. Surely we should daily rejoice at what God has prepared for those who love him!

1. Look up Revelation 21:1–27. The next-to-last chapter of the Bible gives us a prophetic and symbolic glimpse of what happens at the end of time.

1. Bob Geldof, *Is That It?* (New York: Weidenfeld and Nicholson, 1987).

a. What are some specific details John gives us here about the new heavens and the new earth? Who is there? What are they doing? Who is not there?

b. God depicts for us, in this chapter of Revelation and the next, "paradise restored." What are some of the things restored from the fall in the garden? Can you see parallels between the first two chapters of the Bible and some of the details John gives us here?

c. Revelation was written to a group of persecuted and suffering churches, by and large. How would this closing vision have given them hope? How does it give us hope?

d. In these verses, we get a glimpse of a restored creation. This has begun now, in our lives as Christians and in the church. What does this coming restoration teach us about how Christians should treat the environment? Other people?

e. John says that "nothing impure will enter" but only those "written in the Lamb's book of life" (v. 27). What does this verse teach us about salvation and God's sovereignty? Is the idea of hell beneath the surface in this verse? How is such a place compatible with the new heavens and the new earth (see Rev. 14:11)?

2. Look up 2 Corinthians 5:1–10. Paul speaks in these verses about the resurrection body.

a. What does Paul mean by "this tent"? What does it mean to be "further clothed"?

b. What is the practical outcome, for Paul, of knowing that we have a resurrection body awaiting us and the promise of God to guarantee this glory? How does it cause him and his fellow laborers to live?

c. What does Paul mean when he writes, "We would prefer to be away from the body and at home with the Lord"? How does this view of our present life affect how we look at things like money, possessions, and time?

    d. The last verse of this passage is striking: what we do in this life matters. Why would what we do with our present have such an impact on our future life? What does the resurrection of the body teach us about our "use" of our present bodies?

3. Look up Romans 8:18–25. In chapter 8, Paul is detailing the work of the Holy Spirit.

    a. Why does Paul connect present suffering and future glory (v. 18)?

    b. What does Paul mean by the creation "groaning"? How does the creation groan in this present age?

    c. How does he connect the groaning of creation with the groaning of individual Christians? What does this teach us about what to expect in this life?

    d. People often struggle with the fact that they cannot see God and that almost every single benefit promised to the believer awaits future perfection. What does Paul's teaching about hope in verses 24–25 reveal to us about the focus of our hope? How can we have hope in what we do not see?

4. We have studied the Apostles' Creed thoroughly together. How do these great truths contained in the creed give us the answers so many people are searching for? How can you use the creed to reach out to people who seem hopeless?

For Further Reading

Cross, Timothy. *I Believe: The Apostles' Creed Simply Explained.* Leominster: Day One Publications, 2010.

Ferguson, Sinclair B. *The Holy Spirit.* Downers Grove, IL: IVP Academic, 1997.

Frame, John M. *Worship in Spirit and Truth.* Phillipsburg, NJ: P&R Publishing, 1996.

Griffiths, Michael. *Cinderella with Amnesia: A Restatement in Contemporary Terms of the Biblical Doctrine of the Church.* Downers Grove, IL: InterVarsity Press, 1975.

Horton, Michael. *We Believe: Recovering the Essentials of the Apostles' Creed.* Nashville: Word Publishing, 1998.

Letham, Robert. *The Holy Trinity: In Scripture, History, Theology, and Worship.* Phillipsburg, NJ: P&R Publishing, 2004.

McGrath, Alister *Affirming Your Faith.* Leicester : InterVarsity Press, 1991.

McLeod, Donald. *The Person of Christ.* Downers Grove, IL: IVP Academic, 1998.

Olevianus, Casper. *An Exposition of the Apostles' Creed.* Translated by Lyle D. Bierma. Grand Rapids: Reformation Heritage Books, 2008.

Packer, J. I. *Affirming the Apostles' Creed.* Wheaton, IL: Crossway Books, 2008.

_____. *I Want to Be a Christian.* Eastbourne, UK: Kingsway Publications, 1977.

Philip, George M. *The Apostles' Creed: What Christians Should Always Believe.* Fearn, Tain, Great Britain: Christian Focus Publications, 1997.

Schaff, Philip. *The Creeds of Christendom, with a History and Critical Notes.* New York: Harper and Brothers, 1877.

Venema, Cornelis P. *What We Believe: An Exposition of the Apostles' Creed*. Grandville, MI: Reformed Fellowship Inc., 1996.

Wells, David. *God in the Wasteland: The Reality of Truth in a World of Fading Dreams*. Grand Rapids: Eerdmans, 1994.

Witsius, Herman. *Sacred Dissertations on What Is Commonly Called the Apostles' Creed*. Translated by Donald Fraser. Escondido CA: The den Dulk Christian Foundation, 1993.